The new liberty

Ralf Dahrendorf

The new liberty

Survival and justice in a changing world

The Reith Lectures

Stanford University Press
Stanford, California
1975

Stanford University Press. Stanford, California
© *1975 by Ralf Dahrendorf*
Originating publisher :
Routledge & Kegan Paul Ltd., London, 1975
Printed in the United States of America
ISBN 0–8047–0882–7
LC 75–186

Contents

Preface

There is nothing quite like the BBC Reith Lectures as a lesson in imperfection. I mean the imperfection of the author of course, but this undoubtedly tells on the result. When I had recorded one of the early lectures, my producer emerged from the control room into what the Corporation somewhat euphemistically calls a studio to say that he thought the recording was pretty good, but how did I feel about doing it again at some other time. What he was trying to say was that I had failed to put my point over to an audience, which after all has a special relevance for an author who speaks with sympathy of the revolt of the individual: people who listen either by themselves, or in the company of one or two others, and who do not want anybody to speak above their heads, either in the physical sense that he seems to address an anonymous mass meeting rather than attentive individuals, or in the substantive sense that he is really talking to himself, in a private language which only the initiated understand and which is in any case not designed to invite others to take part in an intellectual adventure. If I have still not done sufficiently well in both respects, this is clearly the fault of an author who suffers from a double *déformation professionelle*, that of academic and of politician. But for what style there may be to these lectures, and for much more, I owe a lasting debt of gratitude to Anthony Rendell who has managed to be a firm though just and always arguing producer of these lectures whose advice never smelt of censorship and whose interest in the substance of these lectures has now evolved into a friendship.

One result of this friendly co-operation is that I have re-written parts of the text three or four times, and sometimes added bits, or cut out chunks right up to the recording hour. I must have written a thousand pages in order to produce the one hundred of the final text. Many of these thousand pages are best forgotten, but there are some ideas which I should have liked to develop further, the model of the analysis of change, for example, which is implicit in Lectures Two and Three; or the paradox of a need for devolution in order to allow people to participate, and a need for wider international action to safeguard survival; or the philosophical implications of the discussion of liberty and equality; or a more considered assessment of the doomsday debate. Instead of adding elaborate footnotes on these and other matters to a publication which is not really made for footnotes, I have now decided to collect the materials and addenda on the subject of the new liberty for what may one day become a second, rather bigger book.

The Reith Lectures are a remarkable, but almost awesome occasion to present a mind at work on a subject of contemporary interest. I have felt that I should use the unique opportunity which I was offered by the Governors of the BBC, and in a more specific sense by George Fisher (who manages to combine activity and imagination in a remarkable fashion), in order to try and apply some of my thinking over the last twenty years or so to the pressing problems of the day. Even apart from the opening paragraphs, there is an autobiographical quality to the lectures. In my German dissertation of 1952, I examined Marx's image of the future, wondering why he so systematically refused to admit that this was the future which he wanted rather than just the one which was bound to happen in any case. A few years later, having discovered sociology, I tried to figure out what makes human societies move, and devoted several books to the meaning and the realities of social conflict as a motive force of history. A rather long excursion into politics, from 1967 to 1974, was originally motivated by the desire to make sure that liberty will not be threatened yet another time in the country in which I could do something about it. At the same time, it gave my thinking a somewhat more practical turn; from sociology, I found myself moving towards something which in Max Weber's time was called *Sozialökonomik* in Germany, and what is probably best described as political economy in a sense which has unfortunately become somewhat rare. Experiences in Germany, in Britain, in Europe more generally, and in the United States, have influenced these lectures at many points.

However, it is not these autobiographical elements with their obvious shortcomings and indeed embarrassments which illustrate the imperfections of this little book. It is rather the melancholy fact that all attempts to come to grips with the socio-economic climate of the 1970s, and to offer advice for repairing some of its more devastating consequences, are bound to disappoint a public famished with expectation. Perhaps the public is too hungry, and this is one of the problems. There is too much yearning nowadays for the king who takes us out of all miseries or at least the philosopher who explains them all. Some of the letters and comments (and they were many) which I have received in the weeks in which the Reith Lectures were first broadcast, in expressing either disappointment or appreciation, or in suggesting patent solutions for the problems which I discussed, made me wonder how far the distrust of reason has already advanced. For we may be convinced of the shortcomings of our faculties of reasoning, of applying knowledge sensibly, of convincing by argument, but all other methods are still worse. This, if anything, is the message which I wanted to convey in my own imperfect way.

To call this a book, even a little book, is obviously misleading. Although this publication is much longer than the original broadcast, that is due only to the fact that my own (continental) 45-minute rhythm of lecturing interfered with the 29-minute demands of the BBC. This is therefore the first publication of my full argument, but it is still a publication of broadcasts, no more, nor less. I say this without regret. While I have always held esoteric theory in considerable respect, and regarded it, quite apart from its unexpected uses, as one of the great representative activities of man, I feel that it is as important today to contribute to public debate. If I have achieved this, the education of one Reith Lecturer will not have failed its purpose.

December 1974   R.D.

One

From expansion to improvement: changing the subject of history

The elementary desire to be free is the force behind all liberties, old and new. Indeed, there is little need to explain what this desire is, and some of us have found out about it in ways which we will not forget. I can still see myself, pacing up and down my cell in the prison of Frankfurt-on-Oder in November 1944 (I was fifteen and a half at the time), clutching an almost blunt pencil which I had pinched when the Gestapo officer during my first interrogation had left the room, and trying to write down all the Latin words which I could recollect from school on a piece of brown paper which I had pulled from under the mattress of my bunk. The youthful organization which had brought me into this predicament had been called, somewhat pretentiously, 'Freedom Association of High School Boys of Germany', and it had combined childish things like wearing a yellow pin on the lapel with more serious matters such as the distribution of fly-sheets against the SS state which had now caught up with me. The concentration camp afterwards was a very different experience really; dark mornings queuing in the icy East wind for a bowl of watery soup, the brutal hanging of a Russian prisoner who had stolen half a pound of margarine, slices of bread surreptitiously passed to a sick or an old man; a lesson in solidarity perhaps, and above all one in the sacredness of human lives. But it was during the ten days of solitary confinement that an almost claustrophobic yearning for freedom was bred, a visceral desire not to be hemmed in, neither by the personal power of men nor by the anonymous power of organizations.

The force of liberty, of the principles of a humane and open society, may be equally strong, but it needs explanation, and moreover, such explanation may lead to different conclusions at different times. The series of lectures which I begin today is about the political economy of liberty in a changing socio-economic climate. The new liberty which we can hope and work for, is a liberal response to a world which is in a process of radical transformation. Although the meteorology of the new climate is still imperfect, few people will doubt today that the weather has changed in which we conduct our social and economic affairs. But many have their doubts about the chances of liberty in a world of rising prices, falling incomes, a new distribution of power and impotence, threats of war and starvation, crime and disorder, and declining confidence in the capacity of those who govern, or even the institutions of government. Yet these chances exist, and since they are my main subject let me spend a few minutes disentangling what remains and what may have to be changed about liberty.

As a student of liberty I was lucky to find two great teachers who impressed upon me the two essentials of this principle. One was Karl Popper, the philosopher, at whose feet I sat at the London School of Economics in 1952-3. Popper was, and is, a polemicist who spent much of his time dismantling others, Bertrand Russell for example, Marx and Hegel, not to forget Plato although he allowed Kant and Socrates to escape his devastations. But his message is clear. 'We cannot know', Popper says, 'We can only guess'. Since none of the theories of science can finally be proven right, it is important to continue the effort of finding out whether accepted theories are wrong; and in order to do so we have to maintain the conditions of rational, critical discourse in which it is possible to disagree. What is true for our knowledge holds for our ethics and politics as well. Since nobody knows all the answers, let us make sure above all that it remains possible to give different answers.

This is the assumption underlying the constitution of liberty in all its versions. It tells us that we need checks and balances, rules of conflict, possibilities of change. But there are things which it does not tell us about a liberal order. Mature citizens demand direct participation in their affairs; the new liberty requires the combination of this legitimate demand with the need for stimulating initiative as well as recognizing the order of magnitude of some of the great issues facing us. The progress of citizenship, of the right of association, of the autonomy of many social organizations and institutions has led to a fragmentation of the political public, so that representative government has been transformed into a gigantic and confused bargaining process between organized groups, which leaves the individual in the position of Laokoon rather than that of a proud citizen; we will not have the new liberty unless we create a new kind of effective general public which guards and develops the rules by which we decide on our affairs. In other words, liberty remains a response to the fact that we live in a world of uncertainty, in which nobody can claim to have found the grail of ultimate wisdom; but the constitution of liberty tomorrow is going to look different from yesterday's and today's.

The other liberal essential is social and economic rather than political. Milton Friedman, the economist, is a man who suffers fools, and those whom he so regards, even less gladly than Karl Popper. The year of 1957–8 which we spent along with a number of common friends in the inspired leisure of the Centre for Advanced Study in the Behavioural Sciences in California was coloured by endless debates with Friedman about the need for licensing physicians, the use of the state for organizing social welfare, and the role of government in education. For him, there is of course no such need, use, or role. 'Every act of government intervention', he says, 'limits the area of individual freedom directly and threatens the preservation of freedom indirectly.' And I confess that I am still sufficiently impressed by the argument to wonder whether the collection of rubbish in our cities might not be more reliable if it was left to private enterprise. At the same time, Friedman's obsession with the illiberal potential of government makes him underestimate at least two major issues of the day. The new liberty may well have to be gained not only against the bureaucratic imperialism of government agencies, but as much if not more against the uncontrolled power of allegedly private organizations, giant companies, for example, or trade unions. Moreover, we must raise the question of whether the notions of free collective bargaining, or of the competition of private firms in an open market, important as they are, have as much relevance for individual life-chances today as they did in an economy of expansion. The rearrangement of education, work and leisure in an improving society may require a redistribution of economic power which cannot be brought about by market forces alone. And since I am talking about Friedman, let me just mention that I also wonder whether a technical monetary approach touches the core of the problem of inflation without the solution of which there will be no liberty, old or new.

But when such doubts are voiced, I wish to add that I have no difficulty in following Friedman when he argues that 'the heart of the liberal philosophy is a belief in the dignity of the individual, in his freedom to make the most of his capacities and opportunities according to his own lights'. Friedman also says: 'The consistent liberal is not an anarchist'. I agree; and yet an element of humane anarchy is never entirely absent when the social and economic conditions of liberty are at issue.

The new liberty then is the politics of regulated conflict, and the socio-economics of maximizing individual life-chances But it has to come about in conditions which are so different from those we have seen in the past that an older liberal approach is plainly about to lose its relevance. I want to emphasize this point. The new liberty is not an idea which I advance playfully, because it sounds different or appears exciting. We are compelled to reassess the consequences of our principles by the force of things, things human to be sure but inexorable nevertheless. But first we have got to be able to tell what is the gist of the changes which are going on around us. In some ways these lectures are as many attempts to accomplish this task. You can solve a problem only if you have defined it properly, and often its definition is half the solution.

Let me begin with the message of facts; I want to single out two because they can help us define one of the major themes of change. The first is the energy crisis of 1973, or as it is characteristically called by most today, the so-called energy crisis. It began, as you will remember, with the Arab attack on Israel on 6 October 1973. The Yom Kippur war has shaken the widespread belief in the invulnerability of Israel. It marks the effective emergence of the Arab states into world politics. By leading the super-powers once again to the brink of war, it has further accentuated their concentration on each other, and possibly weakened others who were unable to play their part. It has disposed of the assumption that oil supplies can be regarded as a simple function of the demand of the advanced countries. It has added a percentage point or two to the already rampant trend of world inflation. It has increased the instability of international financial markets by producing billions of vagabond petro-dollars.

Yet I have not even mentioned the most important change, the one for which this war will be remembered in many developed nations, which is a change of attitude. Remember the picture of deserted motorways and cities dominated by people rather than cars, the fright and the thrill of the apparent standstill of the machinery of progress. The American historian Fritz Stern is right in applying the much-used notion of 'the end of the post-war era' to the Yom Kippur war, for this era was above all characterized by a socio-economic syndrome consisting of growth expectations, a consumption orientation, the reliance on international prerequisites like free trade and convertibility as well as national ones like full employment and social welfare, a slightly self-conscious neglect, or perhaps the repression, of awkward matters such as pollution, or even the nuclear threat, and other features related to it. The syndrome had been under some attack in the years preceding the Yom Kippur war; by that time, for example, many countries already had a Minister for the Environment, an appointment which would have been unimaginable ten years earlier. There was a growing preoccupation with the siting of nuclear power stations. A succession of monetary crises had shaken confidence in the international framework of growth. Job satisfaction and participation seemed as important to many as

7

greater production. But it was the energy crisis which brought all these things to a head.

Indeed in one sense, the energy crisis appears like a gigantic historical demonstration organized by the Club of Rome, that private group of eminent scholars and industrialists led by Aurelio Peccei from Italy, and Alexander King from Britain, which has studied the predicament of mankind systematically since 1968, and made headlines in 1972 when its report with the telling title *The Limits to Growth* was first published. Did not the energy crisis demonstrate the limits to growth for everybody to see? I want to talk about the Club of Rome for a few moments, for in a significant way it has become a political fact itself, and one which has much to do with my subject. Some popular politicians, such as the then President of the European Commission Sicco Mansholt, have immediately taken up the notion of the end of growth to argue their own case of a return to nature. Others have at least studied it seriously. When Chancellor Kreisky of Austria invited some of his colleagues to a castle near Salzburg in February 1974, to listen to the gloomy predictions of the Club of Rome, the Prime Ministers of Canada and Sweden, the Presidents of Mexico and Senegal were among those who came. And whereas many have criticized the work of the Club, the echo of its mood and of its themes is evident in Secretary Kissinger's speech to the United Nations on 23 September 1974, in President Giscard d'Estaing's press conference one month later, and in many remarks of the German Chancellor Schmidt. Indeed, it appears that the Club of Rome has interpreted the mood of the times better than most.

The essence of the message of the Club of Rome is, in the words of its President, 'that rapid, radical redressment of the present unbalanced and dangerously deteriorating world situation is the primary task facing humanity', and that therefore 'entirely new approaches are required to redirect society towards goals of equilibrium rather than growth'. This conclusion was based on the extrapolations made by an international group of scientists headed by Professor Dennis Meadows: 'If the present growth trends in world population, industrialization, pollution, food production, and resource depletion continue unchallenged, the limits to growth on this planet will be reached some time within the next hundred years'.

The pessimism engendered by such conclusions was so great that even in 1972 Aurelio Peccei felt it necessary to say that the attitude of the Club was one of 'very grave concern, but not of despair'. Since then, another group of scientists headed by Professor Mesarovic and Professor Pestel has undertaken a rather more subtle study of regional and universal trends for the Club of Rome which was published at the time of its Berlin meeting in October 1974. Its language differs from that of the first report, in that it no longer advocates the abandonment of growth, but a transition, it says, from 'cancerous, undifferentiated growth' to 'organic growth'. Also, Peccei and King put the accent on what can be done to remedy existing ills rather than on doomsday prophecies. But the conclusions remain essentially the same. Too many people have too little food and are wasting too much energy to guarantee a balanced industrial development under bearable environmental conditions. The gaps between man and nature, and between developed and developing nations, augur catastrophes which will shake the world. Mankind is, to quote the title of the second report, 'at the turning point'.

The Club of Rome has already made history and so it should. It has defined one important aspect of what it calls the *problématique* of our time in ways which have already been confirmed by events. It has also indicated some possible solutions. I have three critical objections, nevertheless. Despite all protestations, the reports by Meadows, and by Mesarovic and Pestel remain messages of gloom. Indeed the initiators of the Club argue even in 1974 that doomsday prophecy may be necessary in order to change human and political behaviour. I do not believe in this kind of therapy. Indeed I think that the combination between medium-term gloom and short-term thoughtlessness in the actions of some of our leading politicians is no accident: if you have no hope there is hardly an incentive for sustained change. It may be that I am too optimistic, but I would rather try hard and fail than fall in the useless knowledge that all my forebodings have been right. My second objection to the Club of Rome is that it exaggerates the issues of survival to the point of

9

obliterating the overwhelming significance of justice, and of liberty. After all, survival is not enough, what matters is a life worth living. Is it an accident that the word 'liberty' does not appear at all in the two Club of Rome reports? I shall return to this point, for it is certainly no accident that I propose to discuss the great issues of survival and justice in the light of our desire for liberty: what matters is not merely *that* we cope with these issues, but *how* we cope with them.

Then there is a third critical comment. It is true that the Club of Rome has never explicitly advocated the notion of zero-growth. The first report contrasts growth with equilibrium, but adds that this must be global; the second report even rehabilitates the word growth, at least if this is 'organic' rather than 'undifferentiated'. At the same time, there is some justice in the fact that the work of the Club will remain associated with the notion of zero-growth. For the obsession with growth in its reports is hardly less pronounced than it is with those bewitched by the post-war syndrome, the only difference being that one obsession is negative and the other one positive. In many ways, Germany's or Japan's economic miracle and the pronouncements of the Club of Rome are two sides of the same coin. My thesis in these lectures is a different one. It is that we have to change our currency, the subject of history, if we want to solve the great problems of the day in a liberal manner. Of course we need economic growth in order to cope with the problems of poverty and inequality, and even of pollution and food scarcity; but it must not and cannot remain the centre of our attention if we seek the new liberty.

But before I explain a little further what I mean let me turn to the second of the two facts which are changing the complexion of our problems and their solutions, inflation. Inflation is probably consequence as much as cause of the transformation which is taking place today. Like the energy crisis it focuses several significant trends. Contrary to the Yom Kippur war, inflation has not come upon us suddenly. Nevertheless, there is a specific element to it, and the British case (untypical, but so is that of every country) tells the story: it appears that from about the middle of the seventeenth century until the beginning of the First World War (retail) prices fluctuated around the same level. There were periods, usually of wars in which Britain found herself involved, in which prices rose steeply, but they were balanced by periods of falling prices. With the First World War, prices reached unprecedented peaks; but once again they fell, and as in so many other respects the inter-war period turned out to be one of fluctuations, of ups and downs around the golden summer of 1913. By 1948, however, prices had surpassed the 1913 level and reached that of 1920. After 1948, an almost steady annual increase of between 3 and 5 per cent marked the 1950s and most of the 1960s, until a much steeper rise began towards the end of the 1960s, from 6 per cent at the end of 1968 to 8 per cent in 1971 and, after a brief relapse, into the two-digit figures in 1973. Germany of course had two total inflations in 1923 and 1948 which made for a somewhat different rhythm of development including rather less inflation indulgence today; indeed no two countries show the same inflation profile. But in recounting the facts, the basic point about the new inflation comes out with almost universal validity: something unheard-of in its combination of order of magnitude, range of countries affected, and apparently inexorable power is happening in the 1970s.

There is little disagreement today that a persistent creeping inflation of this dimension undermines the foundations of free societies. Politically, this is evident. Nothing confirms the already widespread suspicions about the inability of governments to implement their promises and cope with problems more dramatically than the continuation of two-digit inflation rates despite universal promises to re-establish stability. The social effects may be less visible, but they are no less dramatic. Inflation has become the medium of a more or less hidden redistribution struggle between those who are able to keep pace, because of their market capacity, and those who are not; the potential of this conflict, like all concealed struggles, is nasty. It includes the danger of a return of variants of fascism. Economically, some degree of price stability is essential to a market economy, even as a condition of growth by re-investment of real profits, not to mention the disconcerting fact that market forces

are obviously unable to correct the aberration which they had produced. Another three or four years of two-digit inflation, and the
free world will never be the same again. But before I come to the
question of how we can cope with inflation (and like everybody else
I have no patent solution to offer), it may be helpful to look at
one aspect of the phenomenon which economists do not always
admit.

Despite all protestations, a creeping inflation has become the
medium in which some thrive and others manage to live. Among the
groups which have to far managed to live with inflation are organized
labour and big business. I am not saying that they actually like the
process, but in the absence of solutions for which they would not
have to pay, they have evolved ways of 'exporting' the cost of inflation to others who are less favourably placed. And what is a question
of interest for labour and business, is one of general attitude in the
advanced societies today: an inflation mentality has spread which
makes it increasingly difficult to lend credibility to programmes of
stabilization. The reason why this mentality has evolved and caught
a hold on people is that it is close to the values which have determined almost two centuries of development, and the last quarter of
a century in particular. Inflation is, like so many motivations and
institutions of the world in which we live, a phenomenon of expansion. It belongs to a world in which people expect to increase their
economic life-chances in money terms. Because they have been
reared on the expectation of a permanent increase in the volume
of money available to them, they press for such an increase even at
a time when this is not warranted by an equivalent growth in production. Public services must expand, but there are no resources to
cover them—so the money is printed. Wages and incomes must be
increased, but there is no growth in productivity—so the process of
nominalization by redistribution sets in. Investment must rise, but
there is no increase in effective demand for goods—so a rise in
prices produces the appearance of growth. In this way, a spiral is
started which eventually allows fewer and fewer people to keep the
pace, and that at an increasingly higher price for all. For the crux
of the matter is that inflation is expansion without growth, growth

ersatz in a sense, an alienated caricature of the mentality which has motivated economic development.

Needless to say, there is more to our economic problems today than inflation. It is the combination of inflation, the danger of world recession, persistent strains on the world's monetary system, and a symptomatic investment fatigue which is so worrying. Moreover, there is more to inflation than the empty claim of expansion. One need only mention the rise in raw material prices to make the point. And to complicate matters further, there are many people even in the so-called advanced societies today who have not had their share of the potential developed by decades of economic expansion. We need more economic growth, if only to satisfy the often elementary needs of those who are still living in darkness while others enjoy the lights of prosperity. Indeed, there is a point underlying much of this debate which I may as well make here, so that I can dismiss it. The notion that we do not really have to worry about economic growth, but should instead redistribute the wealth we have already accumulated, is probably as fallacious as the notion that if you redistribute half-ripe cherries between their owners and all others, everybody is going to have his cherry cake. Redistribution without growth invariably means general impoverishment. But when all is said and done, the general point of fact remains: inflation reminds us of the dangers of a mentality of expansion unfounded in the reality of growth. The turbulences into which it has already led the free countries of the world cannot but leave their imprint. And so they should.

Some economists argue that the existence of unsatisfied needs proves that there are chances of expansion which can yet be exploited. This is both evidently true and, I suggest, indicative of an erroneous approach. I want to suggest that the reason why inflation and the problems related to it seem incapable of solution today is that we look at them through the good old magnifying glasses for the short-sighted, and see them in the perspective of expansion. Apparently our imagination does not suffice to imagine different ways of tackling problems. And yet this is exactly what we have to do if we want to cope. For history proceeds by changing the subject, rather than by progressing from one stage to the next, or even by the dialectical motions of doing, undoing and reassembling things. One day, people wake up to the experience that what was important yesterday, what preoccupied and divided them, no longer matters in the same way. We rub our eyes and discover that the way to solve the problem that kept us awake last night is not to do more or even to do better about it but to turn to something different which may be more relevant, more important perhaps, in any case which permits us to make headway. The *problématique* of history follows the same method: a government which had provoked fierce controversy disappears and takes some seemingly vital problems with it so that people wonder what they were worried about before; an institution which has shaped a decade, or perhaps more, is no longer even expected to cope with problems, it is forgotten; a new leitmotiv emerges, such as that of the rational mind in science and society in the sixteenth century or thereabouts.

In the 1970s, we are in the process of one such historical change of subject; or at any rate we have the chance to solve some of our problems by such a change. This change is probably less sweeping than the dawn of modernity, while it is also less ephemeral than a mere change of government. In the advanced societies of the world, with their market economies, open societies and democratic polities, a dominant theme appears to be spent, the theme of progress in a certain, one-dimensional sense, of linear development, of the implicit and often explicit belief in the unlimited possibilities of quantitative expansion. The new theme which might take its place is still uncertain in its contours, although I shall try to define it further in these lectures. But it is not a negation of growth; the alternative to expansion is not stagnation. In fact, the new subject of history is not an alternative in the ordinary sense at all. In its substance it is neither more of the same thing nor the opposite of it. It is different. The motive force of the political economy of liberty in the 1970s is no longer expansion but what I shall call improvement, qualitative rather than quantitative development. While the life-chances of men remain the subject matter of politics and thus of history, their growth must become a question of better rather than more. Dare I introduce John Stuart Mill's pronouncement which is so frequently quoted nowadays? 'It is scarcely necessary to remark,' Mill says, 'that a stationary condition of capital and population implies no stationary state of human improvement.' I quote this, despite my doubts about the desirability of a stationary condition, because it was made by a man for whom every state of human development posed above all the question of liberty. How can we solve the seemingly overwhelming problems of our day in a way which improves the life-chances of men by maintaining their freedom and increasing their liberty? This may sound like squaring the circle, and yet I take courage from the first sentences of Mill's essay *On Liberty*.

> The subject of this Essay [Mill says] is not the so-called liberty of the will, so unfortunately opposed to the misnamed doctrine of philosophical necessity; but civil, or social liberty: the nature and limits of the power which can be legitimately exercised by society over the individual. A question seldom stated, and hardly ever discussed, in general terms, but which profoundly influences the practical controversies of the age by its latent presence, and is likely soon to make itself recognized as the vital question of the future. It is so far from being new, that, in a certain sense, it has divided mankind, almost from the remotest ages; but in the stage of progress into which the more civilized portions of the species have now entered, it presents itself under new conditions, and requires a different and more fundamental treatment.

John Stuart Mill, when he wrote this in 1859, was talking about a different 'stage of progress', but more than a century later, his question may well be posed again and this is what I am going to do.

Two

The liberal option:
a conflict between
potential and reality

In the first lecture I talked about liberty, and why we have to think about it in a new light. A period of expansion, economic and otherwise, is coming to a close; the problems with which we are faced can be solved only if we change the subject and concentrate on the improvement of our lives. In this lecture, I want to look rather more closely at some of the questions raised by this change of theme. Why is it that there are problems recognized by most, and even solutions for such problems, and yet we do not seem to make any great progress? Who is it who prevents our potential from becoming real, and who on the other hand gives us reason to hope that eventually we can succeed?

Let me begin by returning to the twin issues of inflation and the energy crisis which are both urgent and telling. The rise in oil prices has produced billions of vagabond petro-dollars coming up in odd places and cloaks and in the process threatening the world's monetary system, if not more. Indeed, some of us find it hard to live with the absurd knowledge that while one part of the world sinks into mass starvation, another part collapses because it cannot cope with an abundance of money. For even apart from the dictates of pure reason, there are solutions. It is not totally unrealistic to think of a moderate reduction in the price of oil, by which one quarter of the petro-dollars would disappear, thus incidentally saving some countries from bankruptcy; a further quarter could disappear if a concerted and world-wide policy of energy conservation was adopted, which would also help to delay the moment at which the world reaches the limits of its usable energy supply; a third quarter might well be added to the United Nations fund for the compensation of the poorest of the poor; and the remaining quarter, twenty billion dollars or so per year, would still enable the oil-producing countries to join the club of the rich before long, and what is more, the club would still be there for them to join. Even if such a line is adopted, however, the years immediately ahead of us will show a deterioration of balance of payments problems, continued economic uncertainty, nationally and internationally, and growing differences between countries. But without some such scheme we are heading for a collapse without parallel, affecting not merely the free world but all countries in varying degrees. Why then are we not doing more about it?

Or take inflation. I have argued that some groups can live with the creeping inflation which we have known in the last five years or so, and indeed turn it to their advantage; but even they are hardly happy with the prospect. Everybody condemns inflation, because people feel it in their bones that they are living on a powder keg which might blow up at any moment. Moreover, economists tell us that in theory the problem is capable of solution. They have their differing views, as usual, but the basic elements of a feasible anti-inflation policy are known. A true social contract involving not merely the unions, but all those responsible for determining prices, and incomes, and the spending of public money, is not entirely out of the question; and while the idea of a moratorium on all price and income increases and on printing money, for say two years may seem far-fetched at the moment, it is not an absurd idea. Before such measures would become effective, things will clearly get worse; but if we do not agree on some such mixture of painful decisions, the breakdown of our economies, politics and societies is but a matter of time. Why then are we not doing more about it?

The economic predicament of energy crisis, inflation and the rest is both urgent in itself and an illustration of a more general case. The case could be made for every one of the great issues of survival which the Club of Rome, and many others apart from it have pointed up in the last decade; it is this: we know the facts and the seriousness of their implications; we also know, at least in principle, what can and what needs to be done to solve problems; indeed incipient solutions for many problems have been tried in the last decade; these are somewhat discouraging because it is clear today that things will get worse before they can get better; but unless we do something drastic soon, they will deteriorate until they get out of hand, and threaten our prosperity, our liberty, and ultimately our survival.

This may sound abstract, but in fact it is not. Take the great issues of survival, every one of which bears out the point. Short of unforeseen catastrophes the population of the planet will inevitably double between now and the turn of the century; a combination of concerted birth control action, a world programme for stepping up agricultural production, and an increase in living standards in developing countries might produce a feasible equilibrium at some point; efforts along these lines are made, but at the World Population Conference in Bucharest those who need them most have also denounced them as neo-colonialism. We have entered the nuclear age with its immense military dangers as well as those of terrorism and accident in peaceful applications; unless we control military development and regulate peaceful nuclear advances effectively, mankind may well destroy itself; SALT and the Soviet-American nuclear agreement, the Non-Proliferation Treaty, regional agreements on safeguards and nuclear siting show the way; but the armament race continues. India will not be the last country to have what its politicians cynically call a 'PNE', a 'peaceful nuclear explosion', and if Switzerland, Germany and France continue to ignore the need for a concerted policy of nuclear siting, they will manage to heat up the Rhine until no fish will survive in the river, nor the wine that goes with it on the hills along its banks; in this respect too the hazards are bound to increase in the next decade, but they will become too big for us unless we act soon. The Rhine is but one example of the environmental threat which affects those who live under the skies over the Ruhr or the North of England as it does those who suffer from industrial diseases and ultimately everybody in an uninhabitable earth; important developments have begun such as the work of the Committee on the Challenges of Modern Society in NATO or the Baltic Sea Convention or ambitious national programmes like the one inaugurated by Daniel P. Moynihan in the USA; but already efforts slacken, President Ford announces a return to the priority of growth, and human survival is put in jeopardy. Our resources are ultimately limited, however great possibilities of substitution may be, we live in a finite world; a combination of a strict policy of conservation and an enormous effort to develop processes of recycling used resources from newsprint to rubbish could make a real difference; but already countries begin to repress the shocks of the last years and follow the mirage of wasteful expansion again. Let me not tire you with a list, every item of which is going to rob us of our sleep before long; let me simply repeat: the survival of mankind is in jeopardy.

In this predicament it is not very helpful to fall victim either to the portly pessimism of Robert Heilbroner's claim that 'the hope that can be held out for [man's] future prospect seems to be very slim indeed', or to the sublime cynicism of John Maddox who holds the doomsday syndrome to be short-sighted in view of the fact that man has always coped with his problems and will continue to do so until 'the ultimate disaster, remote though it may be, will come within the transformation due eventually to take place within the sun'. It is no excuse that whatever we do things will get worse before they get better, for we have the knowledge, the technical potential, and even the psychological climate to do something about our problems. Why then are we not doing more about them?

There is a disarming answer to this question. Peachum in Brecht's *Threepenny Opera*, as he wonders why it is that men want to enjoy justice, and peace, but somehow fail to achieve it, finds himself resigned to repeating: 'Doch die Verhältnisse, Sie sind nicht so', that is to say, 'such is life'. Mrs Peachum and Polly agree; I do too but with a different meaning. It is not the human condition which is at fault; rather, it is real conditions created by human beings, and they can therefore be changed.

We are living in a period in which our potential for realizing human life-chances has outgrown the ways in which these life-chances are organized in our societies. We can survive, and we can have more justice, and we can have both in liberty, but our habits and institutions make it difficult for us to do what we could do. And when I speak of what we 'could' do, I do not mean an imagined world, utopia, but the potential of solutions, technical, economic, social, even psychological, which is already there. If we pass through a critical period, it is a crisis of the ways in which we have organized our affairs, not of the capacity which we have developed to cope with our problems. We are, in other words, making it difficult for ourselves to use our possibilities to their full purpose.

This is a familiar line of analysis. Although I have, for good reasons, changed the terminology, it is reminiscent of Marx's dialetic of productive forces outgrowing relations of production. Beyond Marx it takes us back right through the history of political analysis to Aristotle's distinction between *dunamis* and *energeia*, the potential and the actual, or real. Marx, I believe, weakened the thrust of his argument by a specification which proves him a child of his time. He assumed that it was production which determined all things; and while he sometimes used this term rather generously by referring to 'the social production of our lives', he was in fact obsessed with the production side of economic relations, that is, the primary and above all the secondary sector of economics. What he had in mind was of course the fact that the social relations which accompanied feudal agriculture had impeded the realization of the productive potential of industrial manufacture and later mechanized industry. But while this may have been one historical example of how the potential outgrew the real, the contradictions in our condition today require an analysis which is neither confined to one sector of our economy nor to strictly economic developments at all.

There is one other difference of importance. For Marx, the contradictions between existing structures and growing potentials invariably and indeed inevitably build up into a revolutionary situation. The (productive) potential always grows, and the structure (of production) never really changes; the ensuing strain obviously tends towards a breaking point. If this was so, we would have to conclude that there is only one way out of the condition of the 1970s, that is, revolutionary upheavals leading to the sudden, and presumably violent, creation of a new society. I do not agree with Marx here. It seems to me that Marx was blinded by the specific experiences of the French and Industrial Revolutions (the latter in itself a doubtful specimen of its kind), and thus underestimated the capacity of societies to change without drama. It is simply not true that existing structures of social, economic and political relations remain the same over time. We may see, in the 1970s, more intense conflicts and more sweeping changes than in the 1950s. More than that, the ability of our political structures to allow or bring about such changes, may well be severely tested. But there is no intrinsic reason why this test should end in a refutation of democracy by a sudden and violent resolution of the contradictions between the potential and the real. The assumption of a 'system' which is either totally upset or totally maintained, is in fact an analytical one-way screen in reverse: those who look into it see nothing but themselves, their own concepts, without ever even perceiving the outside world which observes them with growing astonishment.

Some people would prefer a revolution to gradual change. I am not one of them. There are times in history when there is no other way out of an impasse but revolt or revolution; these are not times which one would wish on anybody. Quite apart from the horrors of revolutionary periods themselves, the relief they may have brought to some has always been paid for by the suffering of as many others. History is about the life-chances of men, of human beings. This is more than a terminological decision. It is an option against all grand designs which ignore the individual and the simple but all-important realities of his life; it is also an option for the future, moved by a lively impatience with given structures which prevent the full expression of an existing potential of human life-chances; it is a liberal option.

At this point, the obvious question must be raised, what it is about reality that makes it so difficult to do what we should do, and what can be done to overcome the contradiction. And since I am not talking about concepts and their contradictions, but about people and their lives, the question is who, rather than what, represents the potential and the real. If socio-economic structures resist change, it is people who do so because they find that their interests are best served by things as they are. If a new theme is to gain dominance, the theme of improvement for example, and a liberal version of that, there have to be people who can hope to benefit from such change. This of course is the analysis of class which has to complement that of the potential and the real.

Although Max Weber's profound analyses of the sclerosis of bureaucratized modern societies were published more than half a century ago, many people's notion of the dynamics of class is still dominated by more or less vulgarized versions of Marx. Dominant conflicts are, according to this view, generated by economic, especially property relations. On the one side, there are those who own and control the economic potential, increasingly the overlords of monopolistic or oligopolistic enterprises, often multinational, always allied with governmental power, especially with the military complex. On the other side there are those who continue to be disenfranchised, workers, to whom Marxists like to add others today, including many white-collar employees. It is admitted, to be sure, that there are groups which are difficult to place in such a scheme, the very groups of the 'new centre' which occupy the minds of political party strategists above all others today because they can make or break majorities, but in essence, the time-honoured picture stands. It is all the more necessary to take it down and replace it by one which bears more semblance to what is actually happening. For class conflicts reflect the development of social structures: they too become irrelevant when a new potential of human life-chances has emerged.

There is, first of all, the striking fact that capital and labour—or should I say organized labour, even labour organizations—nowadays find themselves not infrequently on the same side of the fence. For one thing, it is no longer altogether easy to draw the line between these groups, either in terms of actual membership, or in terms of vested interests, to say nothing of their part in controlling economic development. But the growing identity of interest which I have in mind is more subtle than the facts that many employers are no longer self-employed or that some workers benefit from profit-sharing schemes of one kind or another. Most shareholders, to say nothing of directors, probably still vote Conservative, and most workers Labour. Wage disputes are often tough in their substance even where they have become civil in their style; trade unionists and industrialists do not often sit on one side of conference tables. Yet there is something peculiar about their contests. At a time of growth without inflation, increases in productivity obviously cover increases in real earnings without threatening profits. At a time of growth and inflation, this is still the case. And at a time of inflation without real growth, capital and labour are two groups which can hope to keep pace with nominal 'growth' and at least maintain their real position. In none of these cases is the dispute between the two a zero-sum game in a closed system—at least in relative terms. It is always others who pay.

Once economic growth begins to be seriously threatened, capital and labour develop a further set of common interests. In the textile industries of developed countries employers and workers have for some time, and with considerable success, been united in clamouring for public support in the form of subsidies and protective measures against imports from developing nations; the tactics have spread to other branches, and with them the thalidomide of protection-ism: to mining and shipbuilding, and of course to expensive high technology projects of national significance. Protecting the *status quo*, the *acqui* or *Besitzstand*, is increasingly a common interest of worried employers and anxious workers; and even forms of co-determination may yet turn out to be what some have always suspected them to be, that is, ways of dissipating responsibility where joining forces seems more rewarding than fighting historical battles. Outside their immediate concerns, in their attitudes to the values of hard work and achievement, to student unrest, to the more costly efforts to improve the quality of lives, to law enforcement, to the assertion of national values, capital and labour have much in common in any case, and the distance between a law-and-order socialism and a conservatism with a social conscience is not very great.

Perhaps we should not be too surprised about this fact. After all, capital and labour are children of the same revolution, ossified though its results may be today, of the same subject of history. For nearly two centuries they were rising social groups. Whatever their problems, they represented the potential of development by contrast to the stagnant relics of the past, to peasants, self-employed craftsmen and tradesmen who were struggling along. Karl Marx confused the minds of many by spreading the myth that the oppressed of one epoch are the potential rulers of the next, and that therefore the working class was going to dominate the future. In fact this is never the case. Even in his own terms Marx could hardly describe the early industrial bourgeoisie as representing the oppressed of a feudal social order. They were a competing élite which had grown up within the feudal society, in many cases consisted of members of the old ruling class, but represented an entirely different potential of economic and social development, a different historical subject in our sense. Is there any reason to believe that the pattern of present and future changes will be different? Capital and labour rose together, they rule together today, and they will decline or at least stagnate and lose relevance together too. Their individual members will no doubt play a more or less important part in the society of tomorrow; but as social groups, the rulers of industry and the rulers of labour are likely to share their fate with the expanding society.

The reality of the expanding society then is determined by the common interests of those with a stake in expansion, the industrial classes, to defend their position. It is also determined by their methods of contracting agreements, as they have developed especially in the last thirty years, that is, by a mixture of false autonomy and sheer power. Autonomy in this sense means dissociation from the legal norms which bind all citizens by defining a separate world of rules; and power is that impersonal version of violence which injures by creating painful conditions rather than by inflicting pain directly. The method has turned out to be infectious, and it has led to a condition in which legitimate government can be nearly paralysed by a chaos of criss-crossing pressures by 'autonomous' groups. But if this is so, who represents the potential of a new, improving society? Where is the competing élite which promises to take over from the rulers of the expanding society? Which groups, indeed classes, are going to determine the world of tomorrow by helping our potential to become real? And what are the conditions which would give these new forces a chance to succeed?

I hope nobody will expect me to come up with a great surprise and produce, so to speak, the *classis ex machina*, the saving social class. This has often been tried, from James Burnham's 'managerial revolution' to the 'scientific estate' of Daniel Bell's post-industrial society; but if we can learn anything from such valiant attempts, it is that they are bound to fail. If there were such a class, we would all know about it, and not just some sociological genius. Perhaps we can do more by trying less, and simply assemble a few significant facts.

One such fact is quite well known, although it is not often discussed. Many eminent members of the ruling groups of contemporary advanced societies have themselves begun to explore new ways and entertain somewhat unorthodox ideas. I have heard union leaders talk about the desirability of a wage freeze, and of more union democracy, entrepreneurs about the absurdity of wasteful consumption, and the legitimacy of demands for industrial participation, bankers and directors of multinationals about the need for rules enforced by democratically controlled agencies, civil servants and other administrators about the primacy of elected leaders and the visible process of decision-making; and indeed a glance at the list of members of the Club of Rome confirms that people can be established and open-minded as well.

It should be said perhaps that many of these unorthodox leaders are more likely to be worried about survival than about liberty. Concern about liberty is, however, widespread among the representatives of the fourth power in our countries, the press, broadcasting and television, the so-called media. This is important, for they provide more than others the missing link between an emergent élite of a new society bent on improvement, and the many who take part in what one might call the revolt of the individual. Forty years ago, Ortega y Gasset advanced his nostalgic plea against the revolt of the masses and for the individualism of an older society. This older society however was one of the few and without the many, and the masses had to revolt in order to assert their rights. Today, many more people have reached the light of civic participation and reasonable social chances. And the plain fact is that a growing number of them are fed up with the new authoritarianism of large and sometimes not so large, but powerful, organizations. These organizations may have helped people to get where they are today, but they have developed their own inertia, and imperialism, until they seem to defend the vested interests of their functionaries rather than the new liberty of their members, while at the same time producing that chaos of pressures which makes effective democratic government increasingly difficult.

Perhaps the student unrest of the late 1960s will one day occupy its place in the genesis of the new process of class articulation which is foreshadowed by the revolt of the individual. It is true that the mood of the young has changed in the last few years. On the one hand, the place of the more colourful leaders of almost spontaneous manifestations has today been taken by bureaucratized cadre-type organizations fighting their sectarian issues rather like some of the anarchist groups in Paris and Petersburg in the 1890s. On the other hand, a large part of the young, and particularly of the students, while no more reconciled with the contradictions and absurdities of existing conditions, is equally tired of professional protest and therefore searching for practical causes. Some unfortunately have opted out to Katmandu.

Nevertheless, as a phenomenon of class, the student riots of the late 1960s must not be overlooked. After all, Charles de Gaulle went down in the May revolt of 1968 in Paris; in the United States, violent and non-violent demonstrations, often organized by students, accelerated the disengagement from the Vietnam war; in Germany, the Easter unrest of 1968 and the subsequent series of manifestations of an 'extra-parliamentary opposition' were one contributing cause of the disillusionment with and, in 1969, discontinuation of the grand coalition. But beyond such specific and national objectives— what was it that the students were worried about? And since not even the fleeting coincidence of Paris in 1968 can sustain the myth of a student-worker alliance—whom do the students represent? Is it conceivable that the rioting students of the 1960s were the Luddites of a new class movement, destroying institutions instead of machines, with the 'Red Danny' Cohn-Bendit as their roving King Ludd?

Students are not very popular nowadays, and their actions since the late 1960s are one of the reasons. Yet they have always had a seismographic quality. Furthermore, they are a part of a much larger social category of those working full-time in educational institutions, to teach, to learn, or to do research. This is a heterogeneous category, and to speak of an educational class is probably a little daring for a sociologist. But class or not, 7 per cent of the electorate in Europe, and twice as many in the United States are living either on or in schools and universities today; and I think it is fair to say that they have something to do with the revolt of the individual against the sclerosis of the expanding society.

The political party strategists of course, in fighting for the 'new centre', have larger, though less well-defined sets of individuals in mind. And indeed, election results from Orpington to Lincoln, from the successes of protest parties like the Democrats '66 in Holland or Glistrup's tax objectors in Denmark to those of Liberal parties in Britain and Germany, confirm the potential of support for the assertion of individual rights against anonymous powers, private or public. But these very examples also show the fickleness of the revolt of the individual; and it would be quite misleading if I were to conclude my assessment of the potential of liberty with the impression that all is well. The plain fact is that many of those whose protest indicates a new potential were the fellow-travellers of a long period of expansion. They profited from it, because everybody did, not because they were in a position to make any effective demands for themselves. Strictly speaking, their bargaining power or market capacity was always low. At a time of slow expansion, coupled with inflation, these groups are the first to be hit. Suddenly, there is no

place left for fellow-travellers, the redistribution struggle which
results from, and to some extent underlies inflation leaves them by
the wayside. The apparently rising groups of yesterday find their
very basis threatened: savings dwindle, pensions lose their buying
power, shares drop, salaries of that important if undefined stratum
between top management and the lower echelons of white-collar and
blue-collar people stagnate in nominal terms and decrease in real
terms, and the same is true for student grants and for numerous
opportunities to supplement income. Yesterday's rising individuals
are today's declining classes. And in history groups which were
worried about their future have been the stuff from which illiberal
politics were made.

I have assumed that the contradictions of our socio-economic
structures will lead to change. Rampant inflation, the consequences
of the energy crisis, the great issues of survival, are all incapable of
solution under prevailing conditions of the relation between government, economy and society. But how can such change be brought
about? The call for leadership has already become very popular in
some places. More and more people seem to believe that if only
those magic leaders appear all will at last be well. Robert Heilbroner
has elevated this demand to a theoretical postulate in his analysis of
The Human Prospect: 'Candor compels me to suggest that the passage
through the gauntlet ahead may be possible only under governments
capable of rallying obedience far more effectively than would be
possible in a democratic setting'. And he adds: 'If the issue for
mankind is survival, such governments may be unavoidable, even
necessary'. There is every indication that we have already begun to
move in this direction. The unorthodox leaders of today to whom I
referred could also be described as the nucleus of a technocratic
élite, and the declining groups of the 'new centre' as one part of its
support. Ideologies of old virtues restored by forceful action are
gaining ground. Heilbroner made matters worse when he answered
his critics by advocating 'a social order built on the model of a
monastic barracks, an army camp. In such a blend of a "religious"
orientation and a "military" discipline there seems to me', he says,
'the model of a social order that, however repugnant to us, offers the

greatest promise for bringing about the civilizational adaptations that the coming generations must make.' China, in Heilbroner's view, 'comes closest today to representing such a civilizational form'.

If this is so, the new liberty which I am trying to define is the opposite of Heilbroner's China. I quoted him, rather than many lesser advocates of cultural despair and a new authoritarianism, because he has misgivings himself; but they make his position no less dubious, indeed dangerous. It is true that the new structuration of classes is ambiguous, and that there are at least two ways of coping with the contradictions between the potential and the real in our world. Orwell's 1984 sometimes seems quite close. I have always felt that 1984 could not last, that authoritarianism was bound to produce a liberal revolt against it, a 1989 so to speak. But of course 1984 should never happen in the first place, and a major item on the agenda of contemporary politics is to resist the beginnings of another wave of illiberalism while at the same time asserting the force of individuals against the new bondage of organization. This requires above all insistence on one guiding principle: on the right and the force of the general public over all sectoral and technocratic claims. It is true that the issues of survival demand vigorous action, often against the entrenched interests of nations and multinationals. Such international action is almost by definition remote and technical, defying both direct individual participation and common-sense appraisal. An effective system of checks and balances in the interest of the general public requires new and imaginative combinations between representation and competence, transparency of motives and control of decisions. A European Parliament copied from national experience is clearly not enough, much less a General Assembly of the United Nations. The issues of justice to which I shall turn in my next lecture require vigorous action as well, often against the entrenched interests of public and private bureaucracies. Initiative, and in this sense leadership, is clearly useful and indeed necessary to make a case for change; but it is more important that such a case be made in a framework which forces people to argue rather than to assert their particular power. Parliament will continue to be crucial in providing this framework; but again it is not simply the parliaments we know which in some ways fail both in their representative and in their controlling functions. Electoral laws, the relations between parliament and organized groups outside, the internal structure of these groups, the independence of the media, the institutionalization of medium- and long-term action, indeed the relations between parliament and government are some of the issues raised in this context. I shall return to them in a later lecture, but only to emphasize the point: what we need to convert the potential of advanced societies into reality is a general political public which allows critical individuals to express their impatience and their desire for liberty in a new world.

Three

Justice without bondage: the liberation of the citizen

The strange tale which I want to recount in this lecture goes to the heart of our problems in modern societies. It is the tale of how the expanding society reaches a point at which all good things turn sour, or rather stale, and all attempts to create justice in fact create a new bondage. For example, we want to break those rigid traditions which confine women to a limited horizon of children, church, and chars; so women are guaranteed equal rights under law; but as soon as these rights are granted, they are threatened by a new rigidity which forces every government department, firm and organization to have a proportion of women on its staff, or even, like the Swedish Liberal Party, 40 per cent women members on all committees. In this way, we not only jump from the frying pan of 'male chauvinism' into the fire of 'women's lib', but we also programme new contradictions which undo the solutions of yesterday's problems. Let me give an example which is even more central to people's lives. A deliberate policy of full employment is one of the great advances which developed societies have made since the crisis of the great depression. But again somehow something has gone wrong about this principle. Instead of telling people that every effort will be made to provide a job opportunity for everybody, and a nearly equivalent income whenever unforeseen problems occur, there is a tendency to assure people that they can stay where they are. This has absurd consequences like carrying token firemen on diesel trains; but it becomes positively threatening to the very right it provides if the cost of false guarantees leads firms to bankruptcy by inefficiency, and thus produces unemployment.

There are many examples of what I have in mind, and I want to look at some of them rather more closely in this lecture. The expanding society had to solve its early contradictions, and notably those by which many people were denied the elementary chances of participation in the life of society, a minimum income, social security, citizenship rights. A century of socialist demands, pressures, and policies has in fact raised the common floor for all citizens very considerably. But it has also lowered the ceilings, and sometimes locked the doors and barred the windows, so that people are safer but not necessarily freer. The metaphor may be somewhat stark, but I want to argue that the new liberty means that we open the door and the windows wide and redecorate the rooms in brighter colours without ever calling into question the right of everybody to live in them without fear. The answer to a mistaken rigid notion of full employment is not, in other words, the cynical one that a little unemployment will make people work and return to virtue again; it is that a general guarantee of full employment must be implemented by a mixture of social security and incentives for labour mobility. We must crack the ossification of justice in order to give people the chance to be free as well as secure.

In my last lecture I discussed our predicament in terms which were to some extent borrowed from Marx. We have developed a potential of satisfying human life-chances, but the real structures in which we are living prevent its expression; if we want to make full use of our capacity to solve problems and do so to benefit individuals and their liberty we must listen to those who revolt against the established assumptions, and create the general political public which gives them a hearing. But Marx does not help us much at a time which the classes which he regarded as the protagonists of conflict have as much in common as divides them. Indeed this is where the other surgeon-general of modern society, Max Weber, has gone a long way beyond Marx. In a classic passage, written in 1918, Weber reflects on the ways in which men have become slaves of what he calls 'coagulated mind': slaves of machines, and of the machinery which we call bureaucracy.

> In combination with the dead machine [Weber said about bureaucracy] it is at work to set up the iron cage of that bondage of the future to which perhaps some day men like the fellaheen in ancient Egypt will helplessly be forced to submit, if and when a purely technically good, that is, a rational administration and provision by officials is the last and only value which is to decide about the way in which their affairs are to be conducted.

Weber raised our own question of how it is possible in view of such tendencies to save (as he put it somewhat despairingly) 'remnants of an in any sense "individualistic" freedom of movement', indeed how guarantees can be given that there are forces which can check and control the considerable power of bureaucracy.

Weber may have exaggerated the dangers of bureaucratic power. He certainly failed to see the desire of those who are working in the glass-and-concrete towers of administration to break out of the prison of their rules and seek a more liberal world. There are other threats to individual liberty apart from bureaucracy. Yet the phenomenon is important in itself and a paradigm for some of the missed opportunities of modern social development, thus of the agenda of an improving society.

Bureaucracy is of course not an historical accident. Max Weber himself linked the growth of public and private administrations to that rationality which informs the modern world throughout. Calculability, book-keeping, purposeful action, the need to give reasons for judgments, the development and application of scientific knowledge, an extension of formalized legal rules are all processes which distinguish modern societies from those of unquestioned traditions, and which require people to administer them in offices, archives and computer rooms. As the process of expansion leads to ever larger organizational units, in industry, in commerce and public administration, in education, in the ways in which we are governed generally, we have to make provisions for their governance which involve people, bureaucrats. Most important perhaps, the contradictions of an expanding society require remedies, unemployment insurance schemes, health services, town and country planning, consumer protection, and indeed policies for improving the quality of people's lives, plus the financial machinery to collect and distribute funds for such services. There can be no doubt that large administrative facilities have become indispensable. Actually, this process has become so much of a habit that we have accepted it unquestioningly even where it could have been avoided; not all increases in sale are really necessary nor all services which are usurped by administrations. But short of a misplaced romanticism which claims that 'small' is not only 'beautiful', but also feasible, we have to admit that we could not possibly live a reasonably secure and prosperous life without administrative services.

But then there is that disquieting way in which in satisfying the needs of a rational society we become quite irrational, the alienation of enlightenment, one might say. Administrations are there to serve; those who man them are a service class which does not determine but executes policies. Yet in fact this is not what happens. While those working in bureaucracies, public and private, may be quite willing to serve, the intrinsic gravitational force of their functions has turned their organizations into a buffer zone between elected leaders and voting citizens which at once separates and incapacitates both. So far as the heads of bureaucratic organizations, ministers and presidents and sometimes directors are concerned, they find themselves confronted with a variant of the re-entry problem in space travel. It is the problem of the exact angle at which they dive into the thicker atmosphere of the organization while remaining intact and alive themselves. If the angle is too steep, the leader burns up in the organization, becomes a part of it, adopts its mores and fails to have an impact; the bureaucratization of leadership. If, on the other hand, the angle is too flat, the space capsule may be thrown back into space, the leader never actually penetrates the organization but remains an isolated figurehead again without impact, brilliant perhaps, ineffectual certainly; leadership without relevance. And a similar case could be made for citizen participation which is fraught with the twin dangers of corruption by inclusion in the organization on the one hand and ineffectiveness by deliberate distance on the other. We need bureaucracies in order to solve our problems, but once we have got them they effectively prevent us from doing so.

What then do we do if we accept the need for administration, but reject the right of bureaucracy, that is, office power? An agenda for recovering public control and individual rights from bureaucracies, while preserving their service for the solution of problems of scale and citizenship is one of the primary tasks of the search for a new liberty. It involves more than one tough decision: decentralization of hitherto centralized functions; citizen participation in communities and organizations; a reconsideration of systems of tenure for administrative officers; the reduction of hierarchical structures by a strengthening of task- and team-orientations; and other efforts along the line of relaxing bureaucratic rigidity. Weber took it for granted that at least the members of public administrations have a special status as civil servants; I do not. There may be a case for a small senior civil service with a status which guarantees impartiality and expertise; but the remaining 5 (or more) per cent of the population who are in public employment should not be privileged by systems of tenure and additional perquisites which increase their immobility and with it their illegitimate, though often involuntary, power.

The iron cage of bondage into which Max Weber saw the citizens of modern societies ushered is unfortunately made of heavier matter than just bureaucracy. The dialectics of enlightenment is not merely one of rationality by administration; it is above all one of that central social role in modern societies, the role of the citizen. The idea that man should participate in the social, economic and political process as a citizen and as a citizen only is one of the revolutionary advances of the expanding society. In many respects, it is a story of success, that is, of the creation of more life-chances for more individuals. Yet once again the success is thwarted by our doing the right thing in the wrong way, liberating the subject of old to become a citizen, only to lock the citizen into the case of his own perverted rights.

T. H. Marshall, the subtle British sociologist, taught his students (of whom I was one) many years ago that citizenship is not a legal status, but a social process, not something people are given once and for all, but the nucleus of a forceful development. Equality before the law and the civil rights associated with it marked the beginning of this process; but who would quarrel with the scorn poured by Marx over the hypocrisy of a contract between an individual entrepreneur and an individual worker. The legal rights of citizens had to be supplemented, by political rights first, which include the right of association as well as suffrage, by economic and social rights later which give people a minimum guarantee of status. When Marshall raised the question of whether the status of citizenship thus enriched was compatible with inequalities of class, he concluded—in 1950, and like so many others at the time—that 'the inequalities permitted, and even moulded, by citizenship' no longer constitute class distinctions and therefore do not give rise to class struggles but become 'socially acceptable'. In fact the force of his own basic idea was greater than he thought; for today it would seem that there are no inequalities permitted, or indeed moulded, by citizenship.

In 1965, I introduced into the German political debate the notion of education as a civil right. It has since become a standard term in this debate, one of hope and active support in the first five years, one of abuse and rejection since. Educational policy, I argued, was to be motivated not by the alleged breakdown of the traditional system, nor by some vague need to recognize social reality and its pressures, nor above all by an imagined or real economic demand for trained personnel, but by the basic social right of all people to be given the opportunities for which their abilities and their desires equip them. This involves the abolition of legal as well as social and economic discrimination, including above all the reduction of that social distance of information and aspiration which prevents so many children from doing what they can do and wish to do. 'In order to create and to maintain a free society, it is in any case indispensable that every man may be a citizen in the sense of his legal rights, and can be a citizen in the sense of his social condition.' Civil rights are therefore not a matter for constitutional theory, but for practical social policy. I would not wish to retract one word from this perspective today, despite the sobering facts of economic development and the discomforts created by the educational class.

In any case I have always assumed that equality provides the floor of the mansion in which liberty flourishes; it is condition, not purpose; equal opportunities are opportunities for unequal choices. I am not prepared to reverse the case and argue that equality of opportunity is realized only once all social groups are represented in proportion to their numerical strength on all levels of the educational system, and that therefore a deliberate effort should be made to insure such proportional representation. By starving private schools and mistaking the idea of comprehensive education as aiming at integration rather than differentiation, we sacrifice the reality of liberty for the appearance of equality. This has nothing to do with the theoretical argument about heredity and environment in intelligence. Of course an active policy of full citizenship means that we make every effort to reduce environmental handicaps for people (and thus incidentally test the theories rather than conduct ideological debates). But we want to do so in order to offer opportunities; so let us be careful not to destroy them in the process.

The point is of general application. The new liberty will not be won unless every citizen is given access to the varied universe of life-chances in a complex society. The new liberty will be lost as soon as it is won if such access is reduced to irrelevant choices between more of the same things, between rugby and soccer, or classics and mathematics. In other words, there is nothing intrinsically wrong about inequalities of income, of acquired status in every sense. It is true that effective citizenship requires the creation of a safety net below which nobody is allowed to fall, indeed of a basic common status; it is also true that citizenship requires the curtailment of the status of those few whose often inherited fortunes enable them to threaten the citizenship rights of others; but there is, and must be, plenty of space between the common floor of rights and the common ceiling of private power. For if equality extends further, if the legitimacy of social stratification is questioned in principle, two equally undesirable consequences result. One is that invisible inequalities emerge, much less capable of control, much more dangerous for the majority, the *dachas* of Communist party functionaries, or the brutal personal power often exercised by one or two members of so-called communes. The other result of a false egalitarianism is that greyness and drabness, that absence of any prospect of individual advancement or collective change which makes certain brands of socialism the enemy of liberty. All men are equal in rank and right as human beings and as citizens, but they differ in their abilities and aspirations. To deny such difference is to deny life-chances, thus liberty. Social inequalities do not reflect an inborn differential of human claims to a place in the sun; their justification is rather, if they remain within the limits of citizenship, that they provide an element of hope, and thus of liberty. The new liberty means that equality is there for people to be different, and not for the differences of people to be levelled and abolished.

Citizenship of course is not merely about where people stand, but about what they do. It is about participation. And once again the dynamics of the idea have brought about profound changes in the last two hundred years. Take political participation, which is the most obvious case: suffrage was extended from a narrow stratum of tax-paying property owners to all men, then to women, lately to all those over eighteen years of age; election instead of appointment to positions of responsibility has become more and more widespread; possibilities of information and public debate were multiplied by the development of the media; education has enabled more people to take an effective part in determining their affairs. All this, it may be argued, is not enough. The story of civic participation is as unfinished as is that of civil rights. This is true. There are still many pockets in our societies where those who exercise authority do not seem to see the need to give reasons for their decisions, let alone subject themselves to the critical review of active citizens. But as with equality, participation has also produced the very forces which threaten its purpose, and it is these which I want to identify.

In the past, civic participation was generally linked to representative government. This is not a necessary, nor even a logical, link. The citizens of Switzerland have never accepted ·the need for representation, but insisted on direct democracy; and John Stuart

Mill was honest enough to admit that the attempt of the electors 'to convert their representative into a delegate', into somebody not elected to exercise his or her own judgment but to execute the explicit mandate of the electorate, was 'a natural and not improbable' demand. He therefore argued, like so many before him and since (including myself) against theoretically pure political systems including 'pure democracy'. However, if one looks at the classical argument for representative government, one can see why the dynamics of citizenship tends to overrun the principle today. 'Mechanics and manufacturers', says Hamilton in the *Federalist Papers*, are not really fit to be members of Congress, they are best represented by 'merchants', on whom they depend in any case, since 'they furnish the materials for mercantile enterprise and industry'. And Mill's own argument, while somewhat less crude in its bias, is in terms of the need to get 'the uneducated' to 'choose educated representatives, and to defer to their opinions'. There are better reasons for representative government, but today they have to be advanced against a massive trend in the opposite direction.

One aspect of this trend is of course the new move towards direct participation: constitutional elements of direct democracy, the direct election to important offices, 'citizens' initiatives' for many purposes, community politics. This is in my view a healthy and necessary part of what I have called the revolt of the individual against the ossification of reality.

But there are other aspects of participation, including the process of converting representatives into delegates. Often, this begins in a practical fashion. Candidates for offices are severely cross-examined; constituency and party meetings between elections become more frequent; articulation of voter interests creates a yardstick for measuring the 'loyalty' of representatives; incumbents no longer seem to have the traditional advantage over their challengers. In some cities, party locals, student unions, mandated delegation, what German Social Democrats call *imperatives Mandat*, has been practised for some time. And as those who hold office become delegates, it is almost natural that the demand for quota representation is growing. Merchants can clearly no longer represent mechanics; both have

to be represented in proportion to their importance in the population, and likewise women, people from every region and borough,
members of religious groups, ethnic groups and whatever other
categories may be relevant. In order to safeguard the participation
of all in everything, delegate government is coupled with so-called
'parities'; *Drittelparität* (equal representation of professors, assis-
tants and students) in universities, *paritätische Mitbestimmung* (equal
representation of capital and labour) in the boards of industrial
enterprises.

The process takes us back to the theme of this lecture, the alienation of enlightened progress. There is a sense in which the extension
of chances of participation eventually destroys these very chances.
People are given the right to participate, even the positions where
decisions used to be taken, but they are prevented from taking decisions by the same token, and tied to procedures which leave them
less room for manoeuvre than they had as the subjects of constitutional monarchs. Take the case of delegation, or (as Mill calls it)
pledges, the mandate given to representatives. It is certainly right
that those who hold elective office should feel and be committed to
representing the interests of their electors; in the past, the principle
of representation has at times been grossly abused. But mandate
government is absurd in theory and frightening in practice. In
theory, it means that the representative is unable to make any move
without the explicit approval of his electors. Such approval is hard
to come by; it takes time and long, almost interminable, discussions.
The delegate is thus unable to react quickly to new situations and
problems. He is above all unable to give a lead, that is, to introduce
an innovation before it has been accepted by all; he has neither
incentive nor real possibility for being ahead of his electorate. This
is bad enough, for it means inaction instead of action, immobility
instead of progress. In practice, the situation is even worse. For in
fact, little analysis is needed to show that the representative turned
delegate will become the spokesman for a rather small group of
citizens: not the entire electorate but a party organization, not the
whole party organization but the activists who can afford to meet
frequently and for long hours of inconsequential debate. And thus

almost imperceptibly the objective bondage of immobilizing rules and procedures turns into the personal bondage of the power of small groups, a new authoritarianism in the cloak of participation.

The case for representative government is emphatically not that some sections of the electorate have to be represented because they are unable to represent themselves. The new liberty is never the liberty of the few. The case for representative government is that it protects the many against the sectional power of those anti-élitist élites who can make permanent organized participation their business without ever being able to win an election. Such groups are quite rightly worried about the visible legitimation of parliaments and elected representatives generally. The case for representative government is above all that it enables communities to change, to seek new departures, while at the same time subjecting all innovations to the test of citizen support. Participation is clearly central to the idea of citizenship, but it is participation with purpose, and the purpose is change. The permanent participation of all in everything does not serve this purpose at all; it is in fact a definition of total immobility. Such immobility is always dangerous; once societies lose their ability to change they also lose their defences against destruction of liberty by dogmatized error. Immobility is all the more dangerous today when major adjustments are necessary to enable people to survive in freedom. While we may have to reconsider the practice of representative government, and especially the ways in which centrifugal forces can be reintegrated into a general process, I know of no better method to make sure that countries keep going without going too far astray.

Justice in the somewhat old-fashioned sense in which I am using the term, means the good society, the right order of things, 'the first virtue of social institutions' which the philosopher John Rawls further explains as 'the way in which the major social institutions distribute fundamental rights and duties and determine the advantages from social co-operation'. Like representative government, and social stratification, this is not a static notion; the meaning of justice changes over time, and the ways in which it is implemented may in fact give rise to such change. Think of those who fought the battles of the French Revolution, or reaped their fruits, the citizens of a bourgeois, mostly industrial society, whose general public was a club, whose market was a market-place, or perhaps a stock exchange, and whose equal rights were after all the rights of an aristocracy, if one of recent achievements rather than distant heritage. They suspected that this liberty was somewhat incomplete, and indeed the liberals of the late nineteenth century were the first to advocate the extension of civil rights to wider social groups. But their social conscience remained bounded by their self-interest, and justice had to be won against them rather than with them. For a century or more justice has meant that more people seek more rights. The historic achievement of socialist parties and movements in Europe (and of Democrats and Liberals in North America) is the generalization of citizenship. Equality and participation, what is often called the democratization of society, are major, and welcome elements of this great process of change; it has become impossible to think of justice without them.

Yet this socialist process has produced its own contradictions, and the focus of justice is once again about to change. Of course, much remains to be done to make sure that everybody enjoys full citizenship rights; but more has to be done to make sure that in the process these rights do not lose their meaning. The price of a century of social justice is high. Men were poor; they fought for civilized standards and social security; huge bureaucracies and mighty organizations had to be created to achieve this purpose; now men are not longer poor but feel that they are about to become the slaves of the instruments of their advancement. I have made a similar case for other aspects of citizenship: we have become prisoners of our own good purpose. This is no argument against the purpose. Were we to try and turn the clock back in order to bring back the values of yesterday, we would make our problems worse by involving people in false and fruitless confrontations. In part, a defence operation may be necessary to safeguard the beneficial effects of citizenship against the dangers of its perversion by perfection: in defence of a mixed public-private economy for example, or of incentives to individual initiative in politics, society and economy, or of the prevalence of general law over sectoral autonomy. But in the main, it is not defence which I have in mind; it is rather a fresh approach to the problems of justice which avoids the fallacies of socialism as our approach to the problems of survival must avoid those of authoritarianism. The progress of citizenship marks enormous progress for millions of people. The privileges lost by some are infinitely outweighed by the opportunities gained by many. But the equality party has had its day, and the task today is to develop the full potential of a new liberty.

It is clearly not certain that this will succeed. The new bondage brought about by a notion of justice as equality is no accident, but is linked to the type of society in which we are living. In the expanding society, every advance in citizenship—universal suffrage and full employment, educational opportunity and minority rights—had to be prised from unwilling and resistant powers. Unless there are solid guarantees, people do not trust their luck; unless the process continues, people fear that it will be reversed. The liberation of the citizen will not work unless people feel certain that nothing will be taken from them, that a more imaginative notion of full employment will not mean unemployment, that a more flexible approach to women's rights will not mean a return to men's privilege. Unless we manage to leave the age of fear, of a sense of the precariousness of all achievements, we shall not enter a new age of improvement. This is where the economic predicament in which the advanced societies find themselves today will put their entire fabric to a test, if the social advances of the last decades are put in jeopardy, our security will be threatened along with our liberty, and the wrong kind of socialism may well prevail; if we succeed in weathering the storm with the achievements of a century of social justice undamaged, we will have reached the threshold of a century of liberal justice.

Four

On difference:
the small (and
sometimes not so small)
things which matter

To those who have followed me up to this point, the territory which I have traversed in the last two lectures must have appeared not only a little arid, but a curious mixture of familiar experiences and strange, not to say foreign, sights. The reason is simple. I have spoken of our societies, the advanced democratic societies of the world, in rather general terms. In fact, such generalities often mean little. When people pore over a map of the world, trying to pinpoint the place where they would really like to live, or perhaps invest their savings, or merely spend their next holidays, they do not much care about concepts like advanced or industrial or even post-industrial society. Australia is attractive for its open spaces, whereas the American frontier is now closed; Holland seems a safer bet for one's money than Italy where social unrest and economic uncertainty cloud the future; holidays in Switzerland may be expensive, but one is less likely to get involved in a revolution or civil war than around the Mediterranean Sea. People may have other motives, but in any case these are not general, but specific, and since such specific motives have a great deal to do with hope, with chances of life, and thus with liberty, we must not ignore them here.

There is another, an almost statistical point which I want to make at the beginning of a lecture on the small (and sometimes not so small) things which matter: the end of expansion is also the end of the average. Whereas for many years, the development of countries, indeed of continents could be described in highly general figures, the percentage growth of world trade for example, or of gross national products, of family incomes, the consumption of luxury goods, student numbers, and so on, such averages are now losing much of their meaning. World trade may still expand, but it is becoming an intricate mixture of genuinely free trade and barter arrangements between capitalist and socialist, or oil consuming and oil producing, or developed and developing countries. Gross national products may still rise, but the variance between extremes of depression and opportunity is increasing in unusual ways. At a time of general expansion, average figures gave some indication of a trend felt by most. The end of the average means that much more attention will have to be given to differences, to regional or structural policies for example in addition to general economic policy, and that the internal flexibility of societies matters more than their capacity to expand. We will, so to speak, no longer grow out of our problems, but have to cope with them instead.

In this lecture, I want to discuss some of the differences which matter for the future of liberty: differences between Britain and Germany, capitalist and socialist countries, and societies at varying stages of economic and political development.

Comparing Britain and Germany is, as you will appreciate, a rather personal task for this year's Reith Lecturer. Sometimes, in looking at the two countries today, one wonders how it is possible to be fond of both, since they are so different. Each seems to have the virtues which the other one lacks. Britain's ability not to lose nerve in times of crisis is clearly not matched by Germany, which has on the other hand found it easier to make the most of a period of stable expectations; the readiness of Germans to work hard and actually like increases in productivity may be exaggerated by observers, but it is certainly not one of the outstanding qualities of Britons; on the other hand the ability of people to make life livable, to be kind, to abide by rules which give a chance to everybody, to tolerate those who are different, in this sense to give quality to human relations is one of the reasons why some Germans like to come to Britain. There may be less to distribute in Britain than in Germany, but there is also more knowledge of how to improve life: and so one could go on wishing for a mixture of the best of both worlds.

The question which interests us in the present context is rather less susceptible to lyrical, or to metaphysical, treatment: how well equipped are the two countries to cope with the problems ahead, problems of survival as well as justice, and to do so in a liberal manner? In part, this is a question of objective conditions. Clearly, the economic turbulence has hit Britain earlier and harder than Germany. There are reasons for the difference. Britain, once the leader of economic development, has been out of step with the times more recently. It concentrated on redistribution when the unparalleled chances of expansion of the post-war era arose, and it sought expansion when the prevailing mood had become one of redistribution, and inflation. Also, and perhaps as a result, the fear of relapse, of a return to the insecurities of the 1930s is greater in Britain, and I sometimes wonder whether Klondike alone, the banks of Sacramento off the shores of Scotland, is enough to allay this fear. This is where the objective merges with the subjective, with the will to survive and to cope, the resources of human energy and intellect to do so. I confess that in this respect both countries have me rather puzzled at the moment. It is true that Britain has a great record of overcoming adversity with existing institutions intact; but it is also true that the need for a medium-term perspective as a basis for informed action is less generally recognized in Britain than in most other countries of the world. The think tanks of London seem to be almost as unpopular as the Club of Rome. There is a shying-away from the future, and as a result a combination of short-term hard-headedness and long-term illusions, dreamy or gloomy as the case may be, and more often gloomy nowadays. In the end, such sustained dejection produces of course the very results which it claims to fear, if only because it weakens the sense of a need for action. Curiously enough, the effect of the prevailing German mood may not be entirely dissimilar, although short-term hard-headedness obviously means something rather less austere in the Federal Republic. The new German arrogance, a sort of political Darwinism which assumes that Germany is the fittest and can therefore dole out advice and sometimes money to the rest, may yet turn out to be the country's greatest weakness. It is as short-sighted as Britain's gloom, fails to bring about both necessary perspective and necessary action, and may in the end add to Germany's traditional inability to cope with crises sensibly, its history of calling for a leader or at least a grand coalition as soon as unemployment reaches 5 per cent or inflation 10 per cent.

These are still rather personal comments, and perhaps I should try to be a little more systematic in wondering just how strong the liberal corpuscles are in the bloodstream of the two countries, how likely they are therefore not to fall for the illiberal solutions to the modern problems of survival and of justice. In my book on German democracy, some years ago, I tried to define this very special haemoglobin in terms of four ingredients. First, the extent to which societies have become modern—Britain of course had a considerable edge over most countries in this respect, from the demolition of feudal privilege to the generalization of citizenship, but others have since caught up, and I wonder today whether there is not a modernity lag in Britain, a need to overcome privilege and authoritarian attitudes, to break down unnecessary barriers between people, make processes of decision-making more transparent, treat those with whom one works as adults and not minors. Second, the ability of a country to live with conflict—most people in Britain would probably say that if anything there is too much of it, and in Germany the obsession with conflict in government-prescribed school curricula has been a subject of noisy political debate; but it may well be that this is merely the other side of the coin of a continued deep-seated fear of controversy which is always bad for democracy. Third, the existence of a political élite which combines diversity of views and interests with a common sense of responsibility—Germany since the war, with all its miraculous achievements, has failed to bring about anything resembling a political class, whereas this is still a strong point of Britain which has of course much to do with Parliament. Finally, the prevalence of public virtues—this may not be the most markéd development anywhere. The desire for liberty in a country depends on institutions certainly, but as much if not more on the habits formed by people around these institutions. While it may be said that Germany's liberal institutions have still not fully moulded people's habits to be really safe, it must also be said that a certain deterioration of liberal institutions in Britain is beginning to affect people's habits. I do not know how to assess the balance of such observations, much less do I want to offer spurious advice about the House of Lords or the education of administrators. It is little more than a guess therefore if I say that while the chances of survival, especially of economic standards, may be somewhat greater in Germany, the chances of survival in liberty are still greater in Britain. Britain may not win the World Cup of Prosperity, but it might get the Liberty Trophy, and to many this would be more than a consolation prize.

I have not spoken much of the ability of societies to change although the new theme of history ahead of us, and the turbulences which still separate us from it, will test this ability above all others. It is here that the countries of Europe seem to me much more endangered than those of North America, where speed limits do not provoke scurrilous debates about public hostility to automobiles, recycling of rubbish is becoming a sport rather than a sign of austerity, as is energy conservation, and the public debate is about real problems rather than ideological deviations: is this or that in keeping with the principles of market economy or not? Are we changing the entire system by such and such a measure or not? Such debates are not only a waste of time and intelligence, but also an indication of rigidities for which Europeans will pay heavily unless they relax them quickly and radically. Perhaps it would make sense to pose the question again which Werner Sombart raised seventy years ago: *Why is there no socialism in the United States?* Because, he said at the time, people get what they want as individuals and therefore do not need collective action. This, I suspect, is no longer true even in the United States; but it may be true still that in North American societies it is easier to make progress, because there is less built-in resistance to change, less rigidity, and in that sense at least a greater chance of liberty.

I have used the term socialism more than once and, being

European after all, I had better add a word of explanation before I turn to the differences, and convergences, of countries which call themselves, or at least each other, capitalist and socialist. Socialism of course means many things to many people, and there are related political terms like 'social liberalism' and 'social democracy' which I would not consider under that label at all. As a force pressing for equality and participation, for the democratization of society in the old industrial countries, socialism has brought enormous advantages to many people; although I tried to show in my last lecture that it has also produced its own contradictions and has therefore become one version of a conservative approach to things, it has had its day. As a design for the world of tomorrow, an almost romantic vision of a life of solidarity and community, of the individual coming home to the nest warmth of the species (in the words of the young Marx of 1845) socialism has caught the imagination of the young, although it is in my view the wrong answer to the right problem. I shall say more about this in my next lecture. But the most striking, and presumably lasting impact of socialism on the history of man is that a number of important countries, led by the Soviet Union in the European aspect of its Janus head, and by China in the Third World aspect, have adopted the method which they describe as socialism to define their road to expansion.

For this is what such socialism is about: an alternative economic, social and political method to release the potential of growth in modern societies, a political philosophy of expansion. Far from superseding capitalism, and providing a prospect of the future of market economies and liberal societies, socialism competes with capitalism for the same effect. Or almost the same effect, for the socialist method not only does rather badly in this competition, but also involves a number of elements which make all the difference, restrictions on individual liberty, a tendency towards monolithic social organization, a dangerous inability to cope with change rationally. It is perhaps unfair to compare the achievements of the Soviet Union and the United States; a handicap of a century of modernity is difficult to make up. But there is one comparison which is almost like a laboratory experiment, that is between West and

East Germany: one country divided into two, and on two different roads to expansion. From production figures to consumption opportunities, national income to private income, the result is clear; in any case a country which has to lock in its citizens with walls, minefields, and barbed wire can hardly claim to have maximized the life-chances of individuals.

There is more to socialism than lagging gross national products and closed borders of course, and the differences between socialist countries are as great as those between Britain and Germany or France or Sweden. Also, while the simple points about liberty and repression must not be forgotten, an ideological cold war is no more helpful than was the political cold war of the 1950s. Clearly, the countries taking part in the Conference on Security and Co-operation in Europe have a number of common interests, many common problems, and should develop some common responses. Whether these will relate to the central issues ahead, the transition from expansion to improvement, is more doubtful perhaps. But the question will be raised whether socialist countries are any more capable of coping with the transition ahead of all expanding societies and indeed whether liberty has any part in the process. My answer to this question would be no: while capitalist countries will be in a mess, socialist countries will be in turmoil. Let me give my reasons.

It is often said that capitalism is unthinkable without growth. There is much to be said for this statement. The profit mechanism, the private character of investment, the stock exchange, the consumption syndrome of creating needs in order to satisfy them, even the system of free collective bargaining are all based on the assumption that there is more to economic opportunities than the distribution of a given product or even a planned process of gradual development. This means of course that at a time of frustrated growth, let alone a longer-term containment of expansion, all these elements of a capitalist economy are threatened. Indeed, in an economy of good husbandry, thought will have to be given to questions like the deprivation of profit, the influence of the public on certain major investments, and the social contract which defines the guidelines of collective bargaining. But the important fact is that all these developments have already begun. A market system is above all one which allows gradual change, and indeed produces it. The countries of the First World may no longer be correctly described as capitalist, but they have preserved the much more basic value of approaching a difficult transition without programming a total breakdown.

In the socialist countries this seems to me much more doubtful. For one thing, they are obsessed with expansion, and indeed with expansion around industrial (and, though to a decreasing extent, agricultural) production. Central planning links the structure of government to the expansion of production; in the absence of elections the achievement of projected growth rates is the measure of success for dozens of ministers and thousands of officials. The ordinary citizen on the other hand is constantly held aware of this overriding interest, and this in a manner which blocks the escape routes allowed by more liberal societies, orgies of consumption for instance, leisure-time pursuits, travel and holidays, the withdrawal to private life. One of the rigidities which account for the precariousness of socialist countries is their aversion to incentives and the corresponding reliance on pressure wrapped in ideology, one day's production for the national purpose, unpaid of course, in the place of overtime pay, production norms to be achieved by hook or by crook, although not by higher wages and better conditions. The machinery created around these purposes is so big and so heavy that it is much harder to move than the constantly changing structures of market economies.

This is reflected in the class structure of socialist countries. Socialist ideologists claim of course that there is no such class structure This, however, is true only in the sense in which it can be argued that capital and labour have come to stand on the same side of the fence: economic and political functionaries and working people represent the same theme of expansion, and that in societies in which what I have called the revolt of the individual is even more difficult to articulate In fact, the class structuration of socialist countries is more explicit than that of liberal societies. The functionaries are a ruling class in the classical sense, involved in a desperate balancing act—keeping the lid down and letting a little steam out to prevent explosion. This is bound to fail at times, and phenomena like 17 June 1953 in East Germany, the Hungarian uprising of 1956, the quiet revolutions of Poland in the mid-1950s and again in the late 1960s, and the noisy one in Czechoslovakia in 1968, are endemic to societies in which those at the bottom of social hierarchies including labour are no better off than anywhere else, the place of capital is taken by a new class of political bureaucrats, and that of wage disputes and strikes, or elections and changes of government by complex procedures of unwilling adaptation which are always liable to break down. In the absence of the safety valves built into more liberal political and economic systems, persistent demands for individual advance will have to take political forms; if expansion stops in a socialist country, suppression is almost the only response to pressures for more consumer goods, and thus the danger of revolution increases. Whether it will turn out to be possible that the ruling groups of socialist countries permit a development which applies less rigid standards to the non-economic spheres of life, to science and the arts, to the mobility of people, in due course to the right of association and of expression, perhaps even to the political process, continues to be one of the great issues of liberty in our world.

But I must watch my step: for in a lecture on difference I have once again begun to say general things, very general indeed. The end of expansion is the end of the average, but not the end of growth; and in the world of three-quarter-capitalist and one-quarter-capitalist, and one-tenth-socialist and half-socialist countries there are some which have a considerable potential of expansion still, although others which have not. The ability of East European countries to thread themselves into world trade, the success of France in finally shedding its lingering agricultural obsession, the attractiveness of American or German industry for vagabond dollars, the exploitation of North Sea oil are important factors in the situation. Looking at the advanced countries by themselves, it is not true that we have a finished cake, and all we need to worry about is its distribution; although in a more global perspective, there may well be some validity to this metaphor. It is obvious to everyone today that the advanced or developed countries of the world are in fact not living by themselves. Even if they wanted to, they could no longer hope to sort out their internal problems without looking at a wider context. As inflation marks the internal contradictions of advanced societies, so the dollar flood is indicative of world-wide contradictions which affect the chances of progress profoundly.

I am not saying this in order to introduce another plea for the poor countries, and for the many millions of people in Asia, and to some extent Africa and Latin America who have neither food nor shelter nor medical attention, but are born into a life totally devoid of hope. There can be no doubt about or responsibility for this most immediate problem of survival. Yet I suspect the dynamics of world development will not be determined by the beneficiaries of the United Nations Fund for the poorest of the poor, the Fourth World as it is now called. In an earlier lecture I made a point about class which can be applied to the international scene as well: an international class struggle, if such exists, does not mean that those who are down today will come up tomorrow and replace the present leaders; it means that a challenger emerges from within the present structures of inequality who in due course disputes the right, or at least the privilege of those at the top and demands recognition. The strength of such countries is not that they carry the moral weight of the poor and oppressed (although they may argue in these terms), but that they represent a real potential of advancement, of expansion as it were, at a time at which those privileged by an earlier start have reached the end of that particular road. This is the case of the Third World in a new sense, the producers of raw materials, the Arab oil states above all, or some large countries with a favourable mix of human and natural resources, Brazil for example, or Indonesia. The central international question for the advanced world is its relationship with the threshold countries, that is those which are about to reach, or have already reached, a threshold of development which enables them to make headway without outside support.

What should this relationship be in the light of my theme of liberty? What needs to be done in order to turn this new predicament to the advantage of individuals and their life-chances here, there and everywhere? These are largely questions for the threshold countries themselves, that is, how they are going to work out their own processes of expansion. Some will undoubtedly feel that they do not have enough time to seek progress in liberty, and will thereby confirm the widespread prejudice to which John Stuart Mill gave such unfortunate expression when he said that 'liberty, as a principle, has no application to any state of things anterior to the time when mankind have become capable of being improved by free and equal discussion. Until then, there is nothing for them but implicit obedience to an Akbar or a Charlemagne, if they are so fortunate as to find one.' Experience shows that while it is only too easy to lose liberty once you have got it, it is very difficult indeed to gain it if you have started in an illiberal way. Nevertheless I should not be surprised if many threshold countries went through troubled periods of believed needs for control and expressed demands for room for manoeuvre, of internal unrest and instability.

Such doubts do not make it any easier to define a sensible approach by the advanced countries to those on the threshold. Yet I believe that such an approach should be motivated by one overriding purpose: to do everything possible in order to make sure that the threshold countries become members of the Club of the Rich soon. Almost everything speaks in favour of this motive. I see little reason to attack the First World, the OECD countries (as one might say) for being rich, or for being a club, so long as they do not use their wealth to keep others down, or their club rules to keep others out. Surely the idea of the Club must be that at the end of the day everybody should be a member. This has something to do with that all-important force in human life, hope. There is no justice in spreading the wealth of nations so thin that everybody is equally poor, and nobody happy; there is justice in giving people a chance, and this is effective only if the chance can be seen to be real. The promise that people will be prosperous, or happy, can be effective only if some people are in fact known to be happy and prosperous. In that sense, the advance of threshold countries into the Club of the Rich might make a difference even to the poorest of the poor. Then of course, if there is to be any chance for spreading liberty, old or new, to more people this will require the opportunity of developing existing potential, and not holding it down until it erupts in incalculable ways.

I said that *almost* everything speaks in favour of such a strategy quite deliberately. For there is that other argument, interest. While an open Club of the Rich is a nice idea, this is not the way most clubs work. Generalized tariff preferences, which would have helped above all the threshold countries to take part in world trade, were prised out of the great trading blocs with enormous effort, and to the present day the United States has not granted them at all, whereas the European Community built numerous safeguards into its offer. While the notion of a gradual entry into the Club, with a sort of transitional period for testing good behaviour, may be an idea which appeals to some, the countries concerned are more likely to grab what they can get and put others under pressure. Some oil producing countries may now regret the damage which they have done by quite arbitrary increases in price, but they do not regret the demonstration of their ability to inflict damage. The conflict between the rich and the *nouveaux riches* of the world will inevitably lead to a shift of power, a spread of privilege, and numerous adaptations of the principles and procedures of the international economic system as we have known it. Unless we attempt to bring about such a shift in a deliberate and considered fashion, however, it may also lead to the destruction of the basis of wealth for at least some of the rich of today, and thus to the decomposition of the very world to which the threshold countries aspire to belong—yet another chapter of that drama which I have called the alienation of rationality, although one which I hope will remain unwritten.

A discussion of difference is almost by definition inconclusive. Let me present my own conclusion therefore as an afterthought rather than as a summary. The fact that the world is a place full of different and often divergent trends, is a source of conflict as well as richness. I for one would not wish to live in a world where generalizations actually describe every case and averages are sets of identical elements. But for many people the interest in difference has another root today. They have found out that difference means that there may be a niche for them to survive the gathering storm. And they are right of course. Katmandu exists, and it is sometimes quite near, in the Black Forest for example, or on the Scilly Isles, or even in opting out at home, smoking pot, going Hare Krishna. One remembers that notion of an 'inner emigration' with which some intelligent Germans tried to explain their silence during the Nazi years. This application of the politics of cultural despair has always helped the powers that be, illiberal powers to be sure. In my own argument, difference is not a hideout; it is, if anything, a further challenge. The road to liberty is neither a way back nor a way out, it is a way ahead. In following this road, difference must never become an excuse, but remain what it always has been, the practical expression of hope.

Five

The improving society: a new lease of life

The world is changing. The survival of mankind is threatened by overpopulation, waste of resources, by the voluntary weapons of nuclear war and the involuntary ones of pollution. The forces of enlightened rationality seem to have turned against their best purpose. The justice of man's social institutions is threatened, too, by the uncontrolled power of organizations and firms and bureaucracies, by stifling equality and impotent participation. The forces of mature citizenship seem to have turned against their best purpose. And the solutions offered by some for these problems make matters worse: the authoritarianism of a small élite which is supposed to assure survival along with law and order, the egalitarianism of a tyrannic majority for which justice has come to mean that no man must have or do anything which is different. The price for these mistakes is liberty, and it is too high, because liberty alone gives survival and justice their meaning.

This is a grim summary. But my contention in these lectures is not grim, or gloomy. It is, rather, that if we go about the solution of our problems of survival and of justice in the right manner, we can succeed without paying the price of liberty, indeed we can have a new liberty. There is a potential of solutions which has barely been tapped and there are many people who would support such new ways. The break required with engrained habits is radical. It is neither a return to the alleged virtues of the past nor a simple revival

69

of the approaches of the present, neither a conservative nor a socialist approach, nor one of liberalism in any familiar sense. It involves a change in perspective, in the frame of mind with which we approach things, in the theme or subject of history. I have called this change a transition from an orientation determined by expansion to one bent on improvement. What is this new theme of history?

You will expect me to give an answer of sorts to this question, and I shall try. But I do so with a mixture of feelings. I have spoken of Karl Popper and his admonition not to fall victim to the temptations of grand designs which in practice enslave men rather than liberate them; Utopia is always illiberal, because it leaves no room for error and its correction. I have discussed difference, the fact that no two societies are alike, and that therefore any general advice one might give is likely to be irrelevant. I have made it clear also that I have no great surprise to offer, no gadget, no patent medicine, that indeed a distrust of gadgets is one of my liberal sentiments. But having said all this, I also remember a paternal friend, the painter Werner Gilles saying to me many years ago in Sant'Angelo on the island of Ischia that he who loses his image of the future has abandoned his life. Is there not something shameful about men who look forward to nothing, who have lost all hope, and live on without purpose or meaning? The opposite of Utopianism is not an empty and often cynical pragmatism, but a sense of direction which remains open to one's own doubts and those of others, but is guided by an image of the future, of the goal which is to be sought.

Expansion is about quantity, about organizing society in such a way that a continuing increase is possible in output and demand, income and expenditure, people's needs and the means to satisfy them. Improvement is about quality. This begins with small things which are nevertheless not to be discounted, because they improve the quality of our lives. The recovery of cities for people is one example: precincts for pedestrians, underpasses for cars rather than for human beings, restored old buildings rather than new slums. The way people live, the space and the comforts of their homes, provides many other examples. So do the arts, the opportunities for recreation and play, sports, and whatever contributes to beauty and to pleasure. All this, I repeat, is important for an improving society, but improvement means more. It is more than a butterfly which adds a touch of colour to an otherwise drab and hopeless world, but goes to the core of this world, that is, the social construction of human lives.

There is a famous passage in Adam Smith's *Wealth of Nations* in which he describes the blessings of the division of labour. Whereas one man working by himself produces no more than 10 pins per day, and thus ten like him 100, the same ten men, by subdividing the task and organizing their co-operation, will be able to produce 480 times as many pins, 48,000. The enthusiasm of the early theorists of the expanding society is understandable. By breaking up complex work processes into simple elements, and assigning only one such element to each worker, two economic effects are achieved at the same time— an enormous increase in productivity because output rises, and a considerable decrease in labour cost, because the skill required from the part-workers is less. Ricardo, and following him Marx, have added the second act to this drama, the transfer of the subdivided part-work of manufacture to machines which can (or so the political economists of the early nineteenth century thought) ultimately be tended by totally unskilled men. This was a mistake, one of the many myths surrounding the subject of the division of labour and its effects on men. Machines require from those who tend them qualifications which, if anything, are higher than the skills of manufacture; and more recently it has become abundantly clear that it is an advantage, indeed a necessity, to have people who understand not only one small part-process, but to some extent at least the entire process of which it is a part. This is important, for I want to argue that the central theme of the improving society will be the attempt to break down the rigidities of the division of labour. Moreover this applies not merely to the phenomenon in its narrow, industrial application, but to that more general partition of tasks and roles which the French sociologist Émile Durkheim called the social division of labour. Wherever human activities have been subdivided, they have tended to crystallize, to become rigid, so that part-work has created part-workers, and the need for leisure a fenced-off leisure time; the improving society, in trying to relax the rigidities of existing relations of production will have to be guided by the purpose to recover integral human activity against all partial claims.

This is not a plea for returning to a subsistence economy in which everybody grows his own food and builds his own house. It is a plea for a modern industrial economy and society, in which the sorting of men into neat little cubicles, exclusive and definitive social identities, is replaced by arrangements which permit choice and change, in short liberty. Even in 1846 (and using somewhat pre-industrial examples) Marx and Engels complained that the division of labour assigns places to people which they cannot leave, so that man is 'hunter, fisherman, or shepherd, or critical critic, and must remain this if he does not want to lose the means to live'. They thought a society was desirable on the contrary which enables me 'to do this today and that tomorrow, to hunt in the morning, fish in the afternoon, tender cattle in the evening, criticize after dinner, if I feel like it; without ever becoming a hunter, fisherman, shepherd, or critic'.

Let me pursue the larger question of the division of labour in society for a moment and look at the ways in which human lives are socially structured. This structure is in essence around three great human activities, learning, working for a living, and doing pleasurable things, or as the tinny language of the day has it, education, work and leisure. In the expanding society working for a living is the central activity of the three, and the other two are in some ways mere functions of work: education as preparation for useful employment, leisure as recreation from the toils of labour. These facts provide their own question marks for the improving society. But here I have another point in mind which seems to me even more important. Look at the oddly rigid and mechanical way in which we have arranged the three dimensions of human activity. A first phase of life is dominated by the process of education, of socialization and initiation and whatever other polysyllables there may be to describe it. Then, duly equipped with diplomas, doctorates or apprentice's articles as the case may be, people are ushered into life. This means, for the next four or five decades of life, work, a job or vocation, having a place or sometimes a career line within that more specific division of labour which relates to the pivotal social role of occupation. It is well-defined, or at any rate defined in detail, and contrasts all the more with what happens at 5 in the afternoon, or between Friday night and Monday morning, or indeed after the age of 62, 65, 67, whatever the rules are: leisure time. After hours, so to speak, people are pushed into an undefined social space in order to enjoy themselves; this at least is the presumption. Indeed when leisure begins to be absolute, at pension age, they are given a small present, a silver cigarette box, or a photograph of their colleagues at work, congratulated on the marvellous freedom which they have attained at last to do what they want, and then they are forgotten, ushered out of life more often than not. What a strange method to make nonsense of sensible things, and even to punish people with their own achievements!

My presentation is of course somewhat unfair. Whatever the shortcomings of social boxes, like education, or leisure, the expansion of these two at the expense of the work box has brought more life-chances to many people, to working-class children who can now attend colleges, to their parents who can now afford holidays by the sea. Moreover, the mechanical subdivision of human activity does not apply to everybody, not to farmers for example, or to prime ministers, or to many women. But the fact remains that the way in which advanced societies have organized the social division of labour leaves a number of questions unanswered which the improving society will have to answer if it is to deserve its name: how can people be prepared for the other activities of their lives in an environment that is almost deliberately closed off from practical life? What chances are there for someone, who after a period of employment, wishes to learn again, new things, or more about those he was taught before? Where is the rhyme or reason for overdetermining people's work while leaving their leisure time deliberately underdetermined? (Is this not, incidentally, one of the contributing causes to that destructuring process to which we owe so much private despair as well as public violence?) What sense does it make to send people who have gathered much experience and are healthy and willing to work into retirement? None of these questions is new, nor is it impossible to give some kind of answer to them. But I suggest that in order to improve our lives, we must think of education in terms which transcend the mere preparation for things to come, of work as more than an unpleasant duty to be dealt with as quickly as possible, and of leisure as more than the residual time in which people are free to tend their garden, tinker with the motorcycles of their friends, play football or listen to music certainly, but also to be bored, to get drunk, to take their own lives or those of others. The reconstruction of people's social lives must overcome the rigidities of a mistaken division of labour. It is aimed at recreating or creating for the first time perhaps, the unity of human lives, so that the social chances of life promise one continuing process of human activity expressed in diverse dimensions and ways. To break down the walls between what we still call education, work and leisure is the first step on this road.

Take the walls around the world of education. Of course, people need preparation for the diverse challenges of their adult lives, knowledge, skills, habits. Some of this preparation must be geared to occupational requirements: and perhaps more could be done to marry classroom and job experience in this process. The central task of education, however, is not simply to produce spare parts for the economic process, but to develop human abilities by opening them up for varied choices rather than streamlining them towards alleged requirements. This is why the educational preparation of young people should be wide rather than narrow, general rather than specialized, and above all not too long. Evidently, some specialist training must be available immediately following general education. It would be foolish not to develop mathematical or musical talent as it emerges. But the accent of education in the improving society should be on something different: on offering a diversified set of formative opportunities for people with a variety of educational and economic backgrounds at all times of their lives. Education is one dimension of the unique activity which makes up people's social lives.

In more specific terms, this is a plea for recurrent education, that is, for the availability of educational opportunities at any time during life. There are many reasons for this aperture. Some of the courses offered to eighteen-year-olds today who receive them blasé or bored or puzzled would be received with profit and gratitude by the same people five and ten years later. The social sciences in any case can hardly be taught effectively to people whose experience of life is confined to their families and their schools; teachers and lawyers would certainly not suffer from some contact with the ambience of their clients; and the formative merit of the arts seems likely to increase if not with age, then with the extent to which knowledge is actively sought rather than indiscriminately poured over undecided youngsters. Odd as it may sound, it is by breaking the alleged economic function of education, preparation for employment, that education would gain a social function worthy of that description, and contribute to overcoming the mechanical boundaries which divide human lives today.

Let me look at another set of such boundaries, those around the world of work. There are specific problems here of the division of labour and how to relax its rigidities. Work places do not have to be as overdetermined as they often are. Experiments in group co-operation even on the assembly line, in a wider involvement of employees in the organization of work, in industrial participation, are promising. But the more important issues arise at the point of intersection of work and what we call leisure. Contrary to some, I believe that it is right that working hours should have been reduced to 48, 44, 40, and often even fewer hours; indeed I have no difficulty in visualizing a reduction of working hours on one job to thirty. But there is one condition, and that is that such reductions must not be used to prevent people from doing what they want to do. Social achievements are there to determine the floor, not the ceiling, of the mansion in which we live. This is not a plea for overtime work, although nobody should be prevented from doing it. Odd as it may sound, I see no reason why people should not seek a second job apart from the first. There is one very large and important group where this is commonplace and generally accepted, married women in employment, who not only have two roles, but two jobs, that of assembly line worker, or secretary, or teacher, or whatever, and that of housewife. Rather than exaggerate the division of labour to the point of reducing these two roles to one (and without prejudging the question whether housewifery might not to some extent become husbandry) —why do we not accept the principle more generally. Is it not humane and indeed liberating to enable people to break out of the restrictions of a division of labour which assigns them just one task and give them a chance to develop some of their dormant capacities elsewhere? Why not hunt in the morning and fish in the afternoon, or to be less rural, collect people's taxes in the morning and repair their cars in the afternoon, assemble television sets in the morning and go to a polytechnic in the afternoon? The ethics not only of work, but of one kind of work, the cruel assumption of a prestabilized harmony between human talent and social employment in ideologies of vocation is misleading, to say the least. And trade unions or craft associations which decry such second chances as moonlighting or, as it is called in some countries, 'black work', could not be further away from their members, although they make it evident also where some of the obstacles to the improving society are. Whenever I have met people who were pleased and satisfied by their work, they were either devoting far more than the normal working hours to it, or had an opportunity to compensate for the shortcomings of one activity by having another one besides it.

A footnote to this plea for relaxing the rigidities of the social division of labour occurs to me, because it has to do with the boundary between work and leisure. Is it not odd, and in fact silly, how we make our lives shorter by insisting on all having our so-called spare time at the same time? What sort of life is it in which only hairdressers can afford to go to swimming pools on Mondays because their saloons are closed to compensate for Saturday's work? Do we really want to reduce the active week of our lives to eight hours on five days, and perhaps soon on four? Longer shopping hours, the scattering of working hours in general, a fuller use of time in several days, may raise apparent social problems, but poses only minor problems of imagination and would above all open up enormous life-chances to people living in cities, if not to everybody, without making anybody any poorer.

What is true for the working day, and the working week, is also true for the working life, and for a problem which makes a lot of difference to many people, and even to the economy, retirement. There was a time, so I am told, when people were looking forward to their retirement, and the ceremony of saying good-bye to them in their office or workshop was a happy one for them. Today, retirement is feared as much as anticipated by many, and the number of those is growing who almost beg for some kind of employment to continue their hold on life. And indeed, what a cruel thing it is to demand from people to devote their time and energy and often emotion largely if not entirely to a job up to the age of sixty-five, and then, from one day to the other, break all that was dear and important to them and turn them into the cold! And even apart from the cruelty, how wasteful and silly it is to reject, on the basis of a schematic rule, the experience assembled by people over a long working life and start again from scratch. I think it is probably a good idea to fix a time at which it is possible to shift people from positions of responsibility so that younger men and women can be promoted into them; possibly this time coincides with present pension age, perhaps it should be even earlier. But I think on the other hand that every effort should be made to keep the elderly fully participating in the life of society, and to retire them only for reasons of ill health or if they themselves want to be retired. Indeed, this is one of the tests for the ability of the improving society to replace the cubicles of subdivided labour by a field of continuing activity.

There are obvious questions which many of you are bound to raise at this point, such as: can we afford all this? Or: how can such changes be brought about? And I shall say a word about the economics and politics of the improving society presently. But before I do so, I must turn to a less obvious, though more difficult, a philosophical question in this context. It is a question of liberty. In a memorable passage of his *Capital* Karl Marx deals with the very problem which I have discussed here:

Indeed the realm of liberty begins only where work which is determined by need and external purpose ceases; it lies thus in the nature of things beyond the sphere of material production

proper. . . . Liberty in this respect can consist only in that
socialized man, the associated producers, regulate their meta-
bolism with nature in a rational manner, bring it under their
communal control, instead of being dominated by it as by a
blind power; accomplish it with the least expenditure of
strength and under conditions most adequate and worthy of
their human nature. But this will always remain a realm of
necessity. Beyond this realm there begins that development of
human energy which is a purpose in itself, the true realm of
liberty which however can blossom only on that realm of
necessity as its basis. Shortening the working day is the basic
condition.

This is an historic statement, and yet one which involves a profound
and consequential error. It marks enormous progress over the
prejudice of centuries as this was classically formulated by Aristotle
in 330 B.C. He too distinguished between two realms, the realm of
work as he called it, of practice, and that of leisure, of the theoretical
life. But for him, as for so many who followed him over the ages,
there was a natural selection of men; some were predestined to enjoy
a life of educated leisure, whereas others were created to work, to
serve, to do the menial things. There is, so to speak, a class structure
of liberty, more, of the right to liberty; from Aristotle to Augustine
and further to Calvin and indeed to John Stuart Mill this belief
prevailed. Marx was free of it, and to that extent at least was a
modern liberal considerably ahead of his time.

But while Marx overcame the notion of a class structure of liberty,
he maintained the unfortunate distinction between a world of freedom and one of necessity. Or should I say more precisely, he remained in a tradition which makes a principle of the fact that men
can survive without being free, that the necessities of life, food and
shelter, can be distinguished from certain other needs, love perhaps
and certainly liberty, which are less strictly necessary and therefore
subject to different rules. It is true that this distinction can be made.
But it is also true that in making it in Marx's, or in Aristotle's way,
one has reduced freedom to a luxury, a part-time value, a principle

applying only to those things not strictly necessary, the nicer side of life. The theoretical danger of such an approach is that liberty, like leisure in our current terminology, becomes a residual value, something undefined that begins to apply once one has got the time to think about it. The practical danger is even greater. To admit the need, indeed to demand a 'rational', 'controlled', and that is illiberal organization of any part of social life, as Marx does for the realm of necessity, is to allow the virus of illiberalism into the fabric of society. Could one not argue such an approach would justify all the perversions of Marxism which we have come to see since 1917? Is it not the need to organize the realm of necessity which has given rise to that planned rationality in which in time men become so much more enslaved than by a market turned rigid by its own contradictions? Indeed, there is a sense in which capitalism, or its theory at least, marks the second great step of progress away from Aristotle: the insistence that liberty, both in the sense of openness for change and of the primacy of individual life-chances, must be carried right into the realm of necessity and must govern all spheres of life. Liberty is indivisible; whoever begins to divide it has lost it.

What then does this mean for that range of concerns which Marx calls the realm of necessity? How, in other words, does the improving society cope with its economic problems? I am not an economist, and can therefore imagine what members of the guild will have to say about the amateur, or rather dilettante, who ventures into their territory. Let me be duly cautious therefore, and confine myself to one remark. It is that the transition from expansion to improvement is also one in general economic attitudes. I think I have made it sufficiently clear that I am not against growth, and that indeed a great deal of structural, regional and national difference will and should lead to a net effect of growth. But there is a difference between an economy which is largely if not entirely built around expansion as its goal and purpose and one which has the purpose of making improvement possible. I hesitate to compare the productive sector of the economy in an improving society with that of agriculture in an expanding industrial society; the industrial world has never really managed to come to grips with agricultural production, its needs and limits, and either gone overboard in the British direction of external dependence or in the Continental direction of protective self-sufficiency; in addition, a new world market condition finds governments bewildered rather than prepared; but the point remains: agriculture is not the centre-piece of an industrial economy, but is a necessary condition and supplement of its development, and a husbanding approach to cultivating land and breeding cattle has served countries well. What we may need in future is the extension of this principle, an economy of good husbandry in which industrial production serves the other functions of life as agriculture served the industrial world.

This requires a transformation of the economic system in several important respects. An economy of good husbandry would subject its development to public, that is political decisions much more than an economy orientated towards expansion. This means of course investment incentives and restrictions in those areas in which either the size of enterprises or the sensitive nature of production have made the operation of market forces an expensive illusion in any case. In an economy of good husbandry rules would have to be introduced which restrict the private disposition of profits as well as the unfettered use of bargaining power. The breakdown of certain essential public services is as unbearable as the breakdown of food supply. Needless to say, this involves limitations on the freedom of collective bargaining and on the power of giant companies, national or multinational—a code of good conduct at least, a social contract perhaps, legislation if all other methods fail. But despite such rules, there is, and must be, plenty of space for initiative in an economy of good husbandry, and indeed incentive for investment by opportunities for profit. Reliance on market forces is still the most effective way to promote economic development in the interest of individuals; and I have no reason to believe that comprehensive planning is less likely to go astray than individual decisions in a competitive market situation. But reality has moved a long way from such ideal types anyway, and rules are needed to make sure that the ideology of the market, of private initiative and capital freedom, is not abused to defend what is in fact the uncontrolled power of some to prevent the transition from expansion to improvement.

There is an implication to these thoughts which has to be made explicit. Whereas the central institutions of the expanding society were economic, those of the improving society are political, that is public, general and open. I have insisted on this point throughout and I want to do so again with emphasis. An improving society, and economy of good husbandry, requires an effective public, that is a polity which permits both initiative and control. This is not an argument for the simple reconstruction of representative, let alone national, government as we have known it in the past. Indeed the singular 'general public' may have to be abandoned in view of two of the great problems with which representative government is confronted today: one, that organization has become a fact, and that a confrontation between parliaments and trade unions or giant companies is going to find elected assemblies on the shorter arm of the lever; and the other one, that the traditional space of political decisions, countries, or nations, is losing in relevance both in terms of a growing demand for devolution and of an increasing generality of the problems which have to be solved. But if the general public becomes more complex, a mixture between supra national, national, regional and local publics, between elected representatives of individual citizens and representatives of organized citizens, the fundamental principle of representative government remains unchanged: that initiative and control must ultimately derive their legitimacy from the common source of citizenship.

This then is what the improving society is about: a new lease of life for men boxed up in the unnecessary cubicles of an inherited division of labour, based on an economy of good husbandry, and brought about by a political organization in which the revolt of the individual is reconciled with the need for recognizing both the reality of organization and the utility of wider spaces. What, you may ask, has this got to do with John Stuart Mill's reflections on liberty? In what sense is my argument still one about the 'nature and limits of the power which can be legitimately exercised by society over the individual'? I suggest, in every sense. For Mill quite rightly began by defining liberty in terms of chances. No liberal will ever prescribe to people how they should live; it is the very essence of liberty that people should remain free to make their own choices. Mill then went on to the liberty of thought and discussion which is so central to the life-chances of men, that is, the existence of media of varied and free expression and communication. He continued to insist, and again I would follow him, on the need for choice: 'A man cannot get a coat or a pair of boots to fit him unless they are either made to his measure, or he has a whole warehouseful to choose from'. This is a point which I have made, I hope, loud and clear. There remains the question of the rights of society to legislate, and thus to impose limits on individual action. 'George Barnwell murdered his uncle to get money for his mistress, but if he had done it to set himself up in business, he would equally have been hanged.' I hope he would not have been hanged in either case, but the point is important. Not moral purpose, but social interest is the legitimate motivation of social acts. The individual is free to do as he or she pleases so long as this does not impinge on the pleasure of others, and even if he does wrong, it is his acts more than his motives that stand to be judged. Nobody should be forced to scatter his years of education over a lifetime rather than have them immediately; nobody should be obliged to stay on in his job beyond the retirement age unless he wants to. But perhaps, in order to make such choices necessary, it is necessary to impose rules which apply to large companies, or to trade unions. Liberty is a general principle, but it is also one which applies especially to those aspects of life which above all define the focus of human progress. All that remains is thus the last of John Stuart Mill's concerns, the one for what he calls 'applications', or even more modestly, an attempt to give some 'specimens of application'. This I shall do in my last lecture.

Six

Steps in the right direction

This is the last of my lectures on the new liberty, and I suspect that some of those who have followed me so far and who now await the solution of all problems are going to be disappointed. I regret this, naturally, but I can neither help it nor apologize for it. I am going to talk about some of the things which can be, and have to be, done immediately if we ever want to enjoy the new liberty. But as we move from the world of goals and purposes to the world of action, the imperfections of men become as painfully evident as the obstreperousness of existing things. We cannot create an ideal world in one fell swoop; indeed we cannot create it at all, and paradoxically it may be this circumstance which makes it bearable for us to live. For it was not with a sense of regret that Karl Popper pleaded for piecemeal engineering as the appropriate method of progress; he did so, rather, because the opposite method, Utopian engineering, by demanding everything achieves nothing, or worse, leads to illiberal pseudo-solutions cloaked in ideologies of ultimate success. There are other ways of making this point. Max Weber for example described politics as a process of strongly if slowly boring hard wooden boards with passion as well as a sense of measure. The point is important, although it is also incomplete. I am sure that Popper, and Weber, did not wish to say that just any piece makes good engineering. Perhaps they should have chosen another metaphor. The steps which we can take here and now are necessarily small, infinitesimal in terms of our aspirations. But they can be steps in the right direction, and this is what matters.

There is a point in this which may well represent a step in the right direction itself. Politics is, quite naturally, about short-term success. Politicians have to make reasonable decisions, but they also have to find, and hold, support for what they are doing. Elections are important guidelights in a politician's life, because it is through them that they know how far they can go. Some people may argue that concentration on the immediate is more important today than ever; unless we weather the economic storms ahead, and cope with the imminent problems of survival, there will be no liberty, old or new. Yet it is unfortunate if such facts are elevated to a theory. The new pragmatism which has become so popular nowadays, insistence on the immediate as if this were a value in itself, is as unseeing as Utopianism is blinding. Without a vision of things to come, the pragmatist is likely to take us round in circles only to finish by saying that it was not his fault if we did not get anywhere. It is his fault. One of the urgent needs of contemporary politics is to supplement, and correct, the pragmatism of the operators by awareness of medium-term perspectives. Somebody has to look beyond the rim of the saucer in which most politicians are huddled together and tell them what happens beyond their local or even national constituency, their term of elective office, their necessarily and at times unnecessarily restricted horizon.

The problem about politics and a medium-term perspective is less one of finding people who are able to look beyond the rim of the saucer than one of making their discoveries relevant. Relevance here means two things. One is that while those looking at the medium-term need some detachment from the immediate, they must be kept aware also of what is meaningful to those in the saucer. Simulating the agenda for a cabinet meeting two or three years hence is likely to be a spurious exercise. The other point is that there must be an effective method to make those in politics (and incidentally in business and elsewhere) aware of the wider horizon. An occasional meeting between prime ministers and members of the Club of Rome is rather moving but there is not much love. I have spent the last ten years of my life exploring the boundary line between day-to-day action and medium-term thinking, practice and theory perhaps; I have crossed the border back and forth; and at the end of the day I feel that making medium-term thinking relevant for short-term action is one of the great unresolved problems of contemporary life, and that we pay heavily for not having solved it.

What then is a step in the right direction? As director of a research institute in the University of Tübingen I have accepted public money to do research in which governments are interested; but without informal and personal contacts they would never have taken notice of the findings. As an adviser of the *Land* Government of Baden-Württemburg I have had an office in a Ministry from which I could influence legislation; but when I had become a member of the *Landtag* some years later, I would not have liked the idea of such non-accountable advice at all, and I also understand why the civil servants did not like me at the time. As a member of advisory committees, such as the German Council on Education I have taken part in the production of elaborate and even imaginative reports; but somehow I feel that educational journalists have spent more time on them than ministers. As a professor-become-politician, I enjoyed for a while being charged with a somewhat 'academic' approach to things by my fellow members of parliament; but before long enjoyment gave way to irritation, and I found myself sorely tempted to sit down in the saucer myself. As a member of the Commission of the European Communities who could not be deposed by governments, and not really by parliaments either, I discovered the important opportunities for relevant medium-term thinking in international bodies. I am still pleased that I got the Council of Ministers to agree on preparing a project 'Europe Plus Thirty' which is supposed to mobilize the predictive capacity of the European Community and look at the prospects for the next thirty years. Indeed I think that international bodies are well-placed to concern themselves with the medium term rather than compete with national governments for short-term effects. However (and although this is less true of the European Communities than of any other organization), they still have built into them a kind of politeness towards their members, a need to accept national statistical information even if everybody knows that it is misleading, which reduces their relevance.

The important point about the establishment of a medium-term perspective within a political structure is that it must be formally related to the legitimate decision-making process, and at the same time removed from the concerns which restrict the horizon of decision-makers. In other words, it must be statutory, but independent in the sense that the terms of office of those involved are not co-extensive with those of governments, and parliaments. I can think of several ways in which this might be achieved. One is an Office of Technology Assessment, to use a misleading, though recognized term. What is meant here is an office staffed by social and natural scientists who regularly examine government policy in the light of declared purposes and known developments. 'Technology' in this context refers to the translation of theory into practice, and the evaluation of practice in the light of theory. Possibly, some such body could profit from the experience of the German Council of Experts whose economic wisdom, in the form of an annual report to government, has made so much difference to the country. A statutory Council of Medium-Term Planning presenting an annual report to government might be one way of combining a variety of experiences. But I hasten to add that there are other ways of coping with the same problem. Even institutions like the House of Lords, or the French Senate, which increasingly assemble a fund of knowledge, and experience, without making it dependent on the time-scales of governments and parliaments may play the part. It is to make sure that those who are, and should be, answerable to the public for what they have done yesterday and are doing today, do not forget that there will be tomorrow, and even the day after tomorrow.

The demand for medium-term thinking is unlikely to be contested, but you will expect me to say something at the end of these lectures, in which I have talked much about the medium-term already, about the shorter perspective. Indeed I remember a colleague of mine in the European Commission turning to me in some exasperation: 'What you are saying may well be true, but I have to cope with the problem that the olive growers of Sicily will force the Italian minister of agriculture to step down next week, unless we do something for them.' It is naturally regrettable if the Italian minister of agriculture has to resign, although in the end (I would argue) the olive growers will get their due only if somebody comes along who not only tides them over next week but has some idea where they should stand in a year, and even in five years' time. But steps in the right direction are about the immediate future, and I shall do my former colleague the favour of talking for a moment if not about the next week then about the next year or two. For this I want to select three issues, to be tackled immediately but of strategic importance; one has to do with survival, one with justice, and one with the area of intersection between the two.

First, survival, or the renovation of the international system in which we are living. For survival inevitably raises problems which transcend the borders of national politics. When the expanding societies had reached the end of the national tether, they created an international framework to make further expansion possible. Free trade within a General Agreement on Tariffs and Trade, monetary certainty within an International Monetary Fund, the Organization for European Economic Co-operation and later the Customs' Unions of the EEC and the EFTA, and even the political and military alliances of the developed world were all geared to safeguarding opportunities of expansion. As such, they served their purpose; but we should not be surprised if they no longer do so. When President Nixon gave notice to the assumptions of existing international economic arrangements on 15 August 1971, he not only created some difficulties but made problems evident also which run deeper and are with us longer than the measures which he announced on that date. Since then, we have lived to see a strange confusion of events. On the one hand, proposals for the reform of existing international bodies have been followed by a proliferation of new arrangements, like SALT, or the Conference on Security and Co-operation in Europe, or the International Energy Agency within OECD, or the United Nations Fund for the poorest of the poor, or the Conference on the Law of the Seas. On the other hand, countries, indeed peoples, have turned away from the international dimension. In these times of concern about the future, they seek their salvation at home, in beggaring neighbouring nations, and more often than not their regional and local neighbours as well. Rarely have those concerned about international solidarity been more lonely, more remote from any constituency except that small band of internationalists, than today.

This is serious, for make no mistake: I am talking about the short term. Mass starvation has begun in the Sahel zone of Africa, in Bangladesh and South Asia generally. The nuclear threat is more real than ever after India's so-called 'peaceful nuclear explosion', the announcement by the President of Israel about his country's nuclear capacity, and the uncontrolled proliferation of nuclear power stations in many parts of the world. The crisis around the supply of resources and the availability of money is at present leading some countries to the brink of having to drop out of the organized international economic system into what is at best national austerity and at worst chaos. And however much people may like the cosy homeliness of their familiar environment, in all three respects effective international action is the only way to cope. We have got to transform the United Nations Food and Agricultural Organization into what it should be, an instrument to ensure industrial production and optimal distribution of food. We have got to combine SALT and the Non-Proliferation Treaty and the International Atomic Energy Organization into an effective mechanism to control the nuclear threat. We have got to reorganize our financial and economic affairs internationally by drawing on the best elements in the GATT and the IMF, the OECD and the new proposals by the American Secretary of State and others.

I hesitate to go further, not merely because I am now encroaching on the subject of last year's Reith Lecturer who was concerned with the possibilities of 'change without war', but also because I fear that I am losing my audience. Yet I am deeply convinced: boredom with international affairs is in effect boredom with survival, and men may unfortunately die because they were too bored to bother about their lives. Let us by all means make international organizations more responsible, more answerable to elected bodies of whatever kind. Let us make sure also that the solution of problems is not left to the idiosyncrasies of personal diplomacy, but embodied in general rules. Let us realize that in this field we do not start from scratch, but have the experience of remarkable achievements by many organizations to use. But unless we do all this soon, we shall find ourselves in a war of all against all in which nobody can win, and in which those will be the first to lose who continue to indulge in the luxury of sweet dreams about sovereignty and autarchy.

The agenda for international action today is about survival, rather than expansion. In terms of justice, let alone liberty, such action provides little more than a framework of necessary conditions. This is true also for a second step in the right direction which in many ways straddles the national and the international, justice and survival. Rapid action is needed to make sure that essential public services are provided at all times and in all places. In the past, what one might call the feasibility of people's social lives was threatened by individual poverty; and on the whole the expanding society has done well in remedying this. But today, and as a result of the instruments used by the expanding society, the feasibility of people's social lives is often threatened by collective misery: trains and buses run unreliably, rubbish remains uncollected, electric power is cut, mail is not delivered, foodstuffs are in short supply, schools and offices and even hospitals are closed because somebody has gone on strike. Whether accident, international crisis, or domestic dispute, the collective misery caused by the breakdown of essential public services involves an unbearable reduction of human life-chances. Add to this the public services which are not provided at all, or very insufficiently: the policing of international arrangements for example, the transfer of technology to developing countries, the containment and repair of damage by catastrophes, or, nearer home, the supplementation of understaffed services in hospitals, or prisons, the care of the elderly and the sick. The picture is unpleasant, and yet far too many of us have settled down to an indefensible acquiescence about its consequences. This we must not do.

I have spoken of a new concept of public service, which may not sound a short-term matter at all. What I have in mind is a delimitation of essential public services from other services, a boundary line between hospitals and department stores, or the post office and the head office of an insurance company; and a clear commitment that essential public services will be provided at all times. This has many implications. Some are technical: does the siting of power stations really provide an optimal balance of supply flexibility and safety? Others are economic: does the collection of bus fares pay for more than the cost of collecting bus fares? But the most serious implications of a new concept of public service are social. There is the question of strikes. In many countries, it is accepted that doctors must not strike because in withholding their services they endanger human lives; in some countries, tradition prohibits all public officials, including teachers and postmen and tax collectors from going on strike, although they have found other ways of expressing discontent. It would seem to me that a public service contract stands high on the list of political priorities: a commitment on the part of the employers, that is essentially the general public as it is represented in governmental agencies, to make sure that public servants do not fall behind in their wages and conditions of work, and a complementary commitment on the part of employees to abstain from militant action.

This would relieve some of the public squalor by which advanced societies are increasingly threatened; however, in many cases services are not withheld but unavailable. We need people to do the things which we need in order to improve our lives and increase our life-chances. This may well be a task to which everybody in a mature society should make a personal contribution; a contribution of time, not of money. Why should we not ask every citizen to devote one year of his or her life to public service? Since this suggestion is bound to be misunderstood in any case, I shall not even try to defend it, except to say that I am not unaware of the practical and sometimes not so practical problems involved. Let me add that however these may be solved, I am decidedly not thinking of a labour service drafted at the age of eighteen, uniformed and barracked, marching out in the mornings singing martial songs to work up the energy for building motorways, or digging trenches. It is quite possible to be liberal and public-spirited at the same time. There is no need to draft everybody at the same time in his or her life; there can be options for the kind of service which people prefer; they might even scatter their service over different times and tasks.

For I am still talking about liberty, the new liberty of an improving society. And while the steps which we can take today towards this goal will not take us all the way, they should at all times be steps in the right direction. A renovated international system of rules rather than a personalized balance of power is in itself a framework of liberty. A new concept of public service should be designed to overcome the rigidities of present arrangements, and enable individuals to enjoy the possibilities of an improving society. But there are steps also which concern the central features of this society, justice, or what I have called the social construction of human lives. In my last lecture, I mentioned a number of things which can, and should be done in order to relax the rigidities of the social division of labour: the humanization of work, multiple employment opportunities, a flexible notion of retirement. These and other changes are all designed to emphasize that human life in a free society is a continuing process of activity rather than an alienated system of prescribed boxes. If I return to one aspect of this activity of life, education, it is because needs and opportunities for change are particularly evident here.

The educational institutions of most advanced societies have gone. In the wake of the Robbins Report in Britain, and similar reports in other countries, we have come to see through an unprecedented period of expansion, more pupils and students, more teachers and higher pay, more school and university buildings, more research funds and establishments in the last ten years. Today, it looks as if this period is coming to a close. Indeed, there is, at least in public consciousness, a certain backlash. As the economic climate changes, education seems to some an expendable luxury. Also, people are a little nauseated by over-exposure to long-haired students, loquacious professors, and unspecified demands for money, all of which do not appear to have made the world a noticeably better place. This will not last. The opportunities for human activity provided by schools and universities are bound to retain their place in modern societies. But once the temporary alienation between education and politics is overcome, one of the first articles of the peace treaty is likely to be devoted to that undefined thing which used to be called adult education, and is now variously described as recurrent, or permanent, or continuing, or further education.

The peace treaty will have to be more definite of course, indeed it will have to define the ways in which education can be interwoven with the general activity of human lives. In terms of education for adults, this involves a change of subject. In the past, what was called adult education was in part a pleasing luxury, lectures about the beauty of Greek temples at the end of an exhausting working day in a grim office, in part a second chance to acquire a ticket of entry to the next floor of the great social elevator called career. It was in any case a catching-up with things which some had been lucky enough to get more easily the first time round. If education turns to adults today, the objective is different. It is to give people a chance to do new things, a first chance in that sense: to return to the classroom in order to structure their experience of life and work, or to develop possibilities which their lives made them discover, to improve themselves.

This is in part a task for educational institutions. A review of courses offered to those who return with some experience, and many of whom have a degree already, is urgent. This may well be based on the experience of the Open University, which has found that many of its students are in fact teachers and other graduates, or on the tradition of the London School of Economics, which has always regarded the teaching of adults as one of its tasks. The other need is economic, the financial support of post-experience students through secondment. Again, some progress has been made. But I would suggest that far more sweeping changes are in fact possible. I see no reason why the notion of sabbaticals should be confined to a few privileged groups, professors for example, or politicians in opposition. Modern societies can afford a sabbatical for everybody. Short of such a rule, or perhaps to supplement it: why not give every young man and woman a voucher for, say, three years' tertiary, or further education? This right could be used up immediately after school, or later, in one lot, or scattered over a lifetime; it would offer new and relevant choices, and at a cost hardly greater than that of forcing an academic or polytechnic education down the throats of 10, 20, even 30 per cent of all young people straight out of school. Many of the steps in the right direction which I have proposed in this lecture are political steps; they have to be taken by governments, by those who elect them or by those with whom they share their sovereign power. This may sound promising but it is not a matter of course. Power has slipped away from national governments, let alone parliaments: to smaller units, regions and towns and neighbourhoods, to larger ones, the European Community, the International Monetary Fund, to extra-political forces, giant companies, trade unions. Paradoxically, the demand for political action grows as modern societies have become ungovernable, because government has lost its relevance. It may be that we can cope with some of our problems without getting governments involved, but certainly governments can no longer cope. This is bad because it robs the individual citizen of his power to influence his affairs. The most important step in the direction of a viable liberal order today may therefore be the restoration of governability by the creation of a new political public.

I have talked about this subject before, and I can therefore confine myself to a single point. The effective political space of legitimate government is not likely to remain purely national. Government is going to be a more complex phenomenon in the decades to come, and so it should be. It will involve immediate participation by individuals in local and perhaps regional affairs, representative participation in national affairs, and qualified participation in international, and at times supranational affairs. But in all respects, though especially on the national and the international level, there is an immediate need to strengthen an effective general public. The mediation between individuals and decision-makers is more important than ever.

This involves several things. Parliament first, which is going to maintain its pivotal position, and to which all other developments must be geared. Then there is the immediate representation of the general public, by political organizations possibly, by referenda or direct elections of office-holders perhaps, but above all by the media. Every time a broadcaster is fired because the governing body is displeased with his views, or a journalist is prevented from writing because he refuses to join a union, liberty has lost a battle. Every time a newspaper is forced to close down, or a broadcasting station is placed under government tutelage, liberty has lost a campaign. A media policy, that is the establishment of legal rules and economic mechanisms to maintain a pluralist structure of published opinion, is not a notion which John Stuart Mill would have entertained gladly, but it is one which is necessary today in the light of his own concerns. But the creation of a general public involves one thing above all, and that is the recognition of organization. This may sound a surprising notion from somebody who has defended the rights of the individual against the overpowering demands of bureaucracy, and of organizations. But the point must be made: confrontation with the mighty organizations of the day, whether they are intra- or international, is bound to lead to the defeat of national governments and parliaments. People are in fact both citizens, individual voters, and members, a part of larger organizations. However distasteful the idea may seem to the classical liberal, we need a second level of organized interest which is both independent from and related to parliament. In this body the social contract might find its organized expression—an Economic and Social Council perhaps which brings organizations into a structure of general responsibility and makes it therefore impossible to ignore them and unnecessary to fight them. In order to cope with the problems of the day, the general public will have to be different from that of the past, general and organized at the same time, a public of individuals, but not of individuals alone. We have to organize organizations and give people control at the same time if we want to be governable. The first test of our ability to cope will come soon, probably in the two years immediately ahead. Max Weber may have been slightly melodramatic in his choice of words, but his nightmare of more than half a century ago is curiously apposite today:

Ahead of us is not the bloom of summer, but first a polar night of icy darkness and hardship, whichever group may win the battle of the day. For: where there is nothing, not only the emperor but the proletarian too has lost his chance. Once this night slowly begins to cede, who then is going to be alive of those whose lent has now apparently blossomed in such abundance? And what will have become of all of you within yourselves? Embitterment or barbarism, simple dumb acceptance of the world and one's place in it, or the third and by no means rarest: mystical escapism by those who have the gift for it, or who—as happens so often and is so miserable to see—strain themselves into the fashion?

The advanced societies, and especially the more liberal ones, are passing through a gigantic turbulence. It differs in impact on different countries, but everywhere it is a combination of factors. Prima facie, the turbulence is economic, that mixture of unfounded growth expectations called inflation, a changing international balance of power, and a general slump in activity. In the first place, the solutions will have to be economic too: a comprehensive social contract committing all partners to a period of standstill, if not some cutback; international arrangements which re-establish stable expectations at a cost to national sovereignty. But let us not be misled into believing that we can afford to tackle this vast set of problems by itself and ignore the purposes for which we seek more tranquil economic waters. Coping with the immediate issues is a necessary condition of survival, but no guarantee of survival in liberty; solving the economic problems ahead is a prerequisite of justice, but in order to give it a liberal meaning we have to be sure not only *that* we solve them but *how* we solve them.

It is conceivable that the turbulence ahead will overtax the nerves of the crew, or the resilience of the equipment, and that the ship in which we are travelling will break up and go down. Inability to cope in the years ahead means wars and mass starvation, the death of millions of people and the impoverishment of many more. There are those already who advise us to change our course by 180 degrees and try to escape the turbulence by a return to more familiar waters. They forget that it was the course set in these familiar waters which got us where we are today, quite apart from the fact that these waters, while familiar, were by no means undisturbed. If we try to return to allegedly good old values, and begin to abandon the social achievements of the last decades, full employment and educational opportunities, pensions and medical care and the rest, we shall have to start afresh in the early 1930s; and there are many who remember the horrible risks which that involves. It is more than likely that a number of people will get hurt before we leave the turbulence. But we can get through, and it is worth trying. The other aspect of our current problems is the enormous potential of human life-chances which the advanced societies have developed. If we look ahead and allow ourselves to be guided by our potential of progress, the polar night of icy darkness and hardship may turn out to have preceded a crisp spring morning of bright colours and promise.

Some will have found my argument, and its loops and lines of analysis rather involved. I can feel with those who expect a speaker about important issues of our time to present his case in a simple manner which everyone can follow. But the issues are not simple. I may have failed to say what I wanted to say as lucidly as is desirable; but I have never tried to join the ranks of those *simplistes* who are so suspiciously certain of their explanations of current evils: that they are all a question of the amount of money printed for example, or of the loss of parliamentary sovereignty, of a hidden conspiracy, or even of the contradictions of capitalist societies. There is no one explanation of a complex reality nor is there one answer to its problems. Analysis and design cannot be simple therefore; but the attitudes with which we approach them are. What matters most in this world is liberty, that is, human life-chances. They are threatened today by the consequences of our own actions; they are also capable of great new development. To meet the threat, and to realize the potential, we do not need a doctrine of salvation. We have the weapons we need, our minds. Reasoned analysis, imaginative designing and an experimental approach to action form a rational, or at any rate reasonable, triptych which has always served men well. This is the method of liberty; its substance is defined by the new conditions in which we live today. The new liberty means that we have to change our attitudes in order to pass through the turbulence ahead in a manner which enhances human life-chances. This is what I mean when I say that the subject of history is changing; and the change in approach is reflected in the words which we use—new words; improvement instead of expansion, good husbandry instead of affluence, human activity instead of work, and of course one word which is quite old, liberty.

Note

Some readers may wish to look up the two dozen or so quotations from other authors in these lectures. To begin with the most important ones: all quotes from J. S. Mill are either from his essay *On Liberty* or from book IV, ch. VI ('Of the Stationary State') of his *Principles of Political Economy*. As for Max Weber, I have referred to several essays of his which are included in the volume *Politische Schriften* (new ed., Tübingen, 1958), especially pp. 320ff, 547f. The two important references to Marx on p. 72 and pp. 77f are from the early critical piece, *Die heilige Familie* (MEGA I, 5, p. 22), and *Das Kapital* (vol. III, ch. 48, III) respectively.

In the first lectures a number of authors are quoted: Karl Popper from *The Poverty of Historicism* (London, 1957), esp. III, 21ff; Milton Friedman from *Capitalism and Freedom* (Chicago, London, 1962), pp. 32, 34; the Club of Rome from the book by D. Meadows *et al.*, *The Limits to Growth* (New York, 1972), pp. 23, 193, 195, and the second report by M. Mesarovic and E. Pestel, *Menschheit am Wendepunkt* (Stuttgart, 1974), pp. 15, 179ff.

Robert Heilbroner's book *The Human Prospect* (New York, 1974), from which I quoted in the second lecture (p. 110), was followed by a BBC lecture published by the *Observer* on 29 December 1974 which contains his praise of 'China'. J. Maddox's *The Doomsday Syndrome* (London, 1972) takes a different view (p. 23).

The reference in the third lecture is to T. H. Marshall's *Citizenship and Social Class* (Cambridge, 1950). Hamilton made his statements about representative government in no. 35 of the *Federalist Papers*. The definition of justice on p. 47 is from J. Rawls, *A Theory of Justice* (London, 1972), p. 7.

Numerous books are explicitly or implicitly referred to, among them D. Bell's *The Coming of Post-Industrial Society* (New York, 1973), F. Stern's *The Politics of Cultural Despair* (New York, 1962), or such classics as W. Sombart's *Warum gibt es in den Vereinigten Staaten keinen Sozialismus?*, E. Durkheim's *De la division du travail social*, A. Smith's *Wealth of Nations*—but were I to list them all, I would contradict my own intention of keeping this book what it was, a series of lectures.